Glimpses of Jersey

A collection of interesting stories and traditions

John Manning

© John Manning

All rights reserved. No part of this publication may be reproduced, stored in a retrieval system, or transmitted, in any form or by any means, electronic, mechanical, photocopying, recording or otherwise, without the prior permission of John Manning.

Previously published in two editions of The Parish Pump in 1987 and 1989. By Channel Television Publications.

This edition published 1994.

Made and printed in Great Britain by
The Guernsey Press Co. Ltd, Guernsey, Channel Islands.

ISBN 0-902550-53-5

CONTENTS

La Corbiere Lighthouse	3
The Glass Church	6
Black Butter	8
The XIIIth Perquage	10
Seaweed: A Useful Fruit	11
The Clameur de Haro	13
The Picket Houses	14
Green Island	17
The Jersey Lily	19
Grosnez Castle	29
The House of Correction	31
A Cemetery for Animals	34
Cabbage Walking Sticks	36
Janvrin's Tomb	38
The Ormer	40
The Early Grammar Schools of Jersey	42
The Jersey Cow	46
A Cow's Christmas Prayer	49
The Vega	50
Submerged Forest and Manor of St Ouen	53
A King is Proclaimed	55
Fort d'Auvergne	58
Gallows Hill	59
The Channel Islands' First Airport	62
Geoffroy's Leap	65
The Black Dog of Bouley Bay	66
Le Vesconte Monument	68
Howard Davis Park	71
Jersey Races	74
Queen's Assembly Rooms	77
Rocqueberg	79
The Battle of the Oyster Shells	81
Greve de Lecq	84
Pierre Le Sueur and the Bread Riots	86
Croix de la Bataille	89
St Saviour's Hospital	91
Occupation Stamps	93

LA CORBIÈRE LIGHTHOUSE

ONE of the most photographed beauty spots in Jersey can be found on the extreme tip of the south-west coast of the Island. Here, 1,600ft from the mainland, standing majestically amongst some of the roughest seas in the English Channel is the lighthouse known as La Corbière.

La Corbière or La Corbiéthe in Jersey Norman French, means the gathering place of the crows. It is situated at Latitude 49° 10' 40"N, Longitude 2° 14' 50" W, and was the first lighthouse in Britain to be built of concrete rather than stone. The designer, Sir John Coode, chose Portland cement for the enormous task of building a lighthouse at the exact spot where it is said seven seas meet.

Many ships have been lost around these treacherous rocks. The first recorded shipwreck was a Spanish cargo ship carrying casks of wine. It came aground at La Corbière on November 25th, 1495 and, because of the law known as the Droit d'Epaves, or Wreckage Rights, both the ship and its cargo became the property of the Seigneur of the area.

There are numerous legends of fishermen, in cahoots with the Seigneur, luring ships onto the rocks by attaching lights to the horns of cows and fastening their front foot to the ground near the rocks. In an endeavour to release its foot, the cow's head would move up and down, the lights being mistaken by the captain and crew of passing vessels as those of other ships moving on open sea.

Thinking they were too far out from land the unsuspecting crew would sail their ship closer in and so onto the rocks. The legend continues by attributing the swallowing up of the land under St Ouen's Bay, which now covers what used to be a great forest, and the blowing of fine sand over the surrounding fertile land, to be divine retribution on the locals for causing the ships to flounder on La Corbière.

The States of Jersey debated on numerous occasions the possibility of building a lighthouse but nothing materialised. On September 29th, 1857, 71 fishermen from St Brelade, possibly trying to make amends for the deeds of their forefathers, signed a petition to the Lords Commissioners of Her Majesty's Privy Council for Trade, requesting something to be done as soon as possible before more ships and lives were lost.

Nothing happened and vessels continued to misjudge their position at night, ending up victims of La Corbière. On September 20th, 1859, the Mail Packet Express was wrecked. No reason could be found for this catastrophe as it happened in broad daylight when all the rocks were clearly visible. Nevertheless it added weight to the arguments for a lighthouse and eventually Sir John Coode was asked to prepare a design and the resident States engineer, Mr Imrie Bell, who had just finished building much of St Helier's new harbour, was given the task of construction.

The survey of the area was completed in February 1873 and the exact position of the lighthouse selected on May 16th that year. All this coincided with Captain William Ward wrecking his ship *The Fox* on the rocks of La Corbière. Work was started immediately before any more misfortunes could occur.

Excavations began in June and the foundations for the lighthouse were cut out of solid rock. It was decided to transport all the material for the lighthouse, causeway, cottage and stores by sea from St Helier. A small sheltered bay was found where the tugs could anchor and a pulley system was erected with ropes suspended between two rocks, one on which the lighthouse was being built and the other on the shore where the causeway was being constructed. In this way work could progress on both units simultaneously, saving many months' labour. To bring the necessary materials by road would have delayed the building programme, as at the time, there was only a rough track to the headland of La Corbière and horse and carts would have had to be used. Also this would have meant the completion of the causeway before work could commence on the lighthouse.

By November 1873, both the causeway and lighthouse were completed although there was a delay before the lantern and lenses arrived in the Island from the manufacturers. The first trial of the light took place on April 24th, 1874, and it became fully operational on June 1st.

The light, which is 135 ft above mean sea level, can be seen for 18 miles, and the 4,000 watt foghorn has a range of four nautical miles. Originally four keepers were used on shift work to man the lighthouse, but in recent years all the services have been made fully automatic. On May 28th, 1946, the assistant keeper, Peter Edwin Larbalestier, lost his life trying to rescue a visitor from the incoming tide. A plaque on the wall of the causeway commemorates his unselfish act of bravery.

A masterpiece of building, this 62ft lighthouse cost £2,976 to build. The light, foghorn and other essential equipment cost £2,555, the causeway a further £1,606 and the keeper's cottage and stores £864. This comes to a total of £8,001. When first opened, the machinery operating the lighthouse consumed 2·26 gallons of paraffin oil every 24 hours and the approximate cost of maintainance including wages, oil, stores and coal was £170 per year. Today the electricity bill alone comes to £2,000.

The lighthouse has been instrumental for over a century in saving many ships and crews from a watery grave. For the visitors who travel to Jersey by sea every year it is one of the first sights they see of the Island after leaving Guernsey. On stormy night crossings many mariners and passengers, on seeing the welcoming light, have thanked Sir John Coode and Imrie Bell for building La Corbière lighthouse.

THE GLASS CHURCH

THE Church of St Matthew in Jersey was built in 1840 to serve the people in the area of Millbrook who previously had to travel to St Lawrence Parish Church for Anglican worship. A small, unimpressive looking building, St Matthew's would have remained an undistinguished House of God had it not been for the widow of a wealthy English immigrant.

Lord Trent of Nottingham, the first Baron Trent, was better known as Jessie Boot, founder of Boots the Chemist. He chose to retire to Jersey, purchasing a house called Villa Millbrook, two hundred yards from St Matthew's Church.

On his death, Lady Trent decided she would like a lasting memorial to her husband. Their nearby place of worship seemed the ideal solution. She approached the Ecclesiastical Court in Jersey with the idea of refurbishing the church completely in glass. Canon law in England forbids glass to be used for certain parts of a church, but Jersey has its own Canon law, and permission was granted for the alterations. The Right Rev. Cyril Garbett, Lord Bishop of Winchester, into whose diocese Jersey falls, also gave his sanction, and work was able to commence on the Glass Church.

Lady Florence Trent commissioned Rène Lalique, the most famous glassmaker of his day, to undertake the renovation. Born in the French town of Ay in the district of Champagne in 1860, he moved to Paris where he studied metalwork, silver and jewellery-making before devoting himself to glasswork in 1895 until his death in 1945. He discovered methods of achieving different textures by sandblasting and acid engraving and became famous for his use of opaque glass in contrast with clear glass. Rène kept his trade secrets to himself and his unique art died with him.

A. B. Grayson was engaged as architect and the two men formulated the plans which were to transform the small nondescript church into one of the most beautiful and unusual churches in Britain. French and Italian craftsmen were employed for the plasterwork on the ceiling, whilst Rène brought stone from various parts of England—Portland stone for the floor, Bath stone for the walls and Hopton Wood stone from Derbyshire for the lectern and pulpit. The pews and all other woodwork were made from English Oak.

On completion of the stonework Rène commenced his glass masterpieces. The communion table and rail depicts the English Lily with the glass screen on each side covered in Jersey Lilies. The glass altar was made to look like marble and the glass font, the only one in the world, was signed by him. In the side chapel stands a 15ft high cross, two large pillars and four angels, all in glass, which are lit during the services, and the six main windows of the church were ornamented with Madonna Lilies. All the casts and moulds were destroyed because Rène never repeated any of his works.

To complete the church, eight toned bells were housed in the tower on which hymn music is still played before the services, and two manual organs were installed to provide the backing for the choir and congregation. Both organs were completely rebuilt in 1961. In 1970 a Vestibule was added along with a Vestry where occasional services are held.

Rededicated in 1934 by the Right Rev. Cyril Garbett, the church is today visited by thousands of tourists every year. A beautiful memorial to Jessie Boot, the church of St Matthew, commonly known as the Glass Church, is also a lasting memorial to the genius of Rène Lalique.

BLACK BUTTER

TELEVISION commercials try to convince us we cannot tell the difference between butter and margarine. Jersey annually produces a butter which any shopper, chosen at random by the interviewer, would have no difficulty distinguishing. Apart from the complete contrast in taste and texture, this butter looks different — it's black.

Black butter has been made on the farms of Jersey for many generations. It is always a festive occasion and is accompanied by singing and dancing which continues throughout the night. The event is usually organised by at least two farmers who, joining forces, pool their manpower and ingredients. From 1940 to 1945, when the Germans occupied the Channel Islands, many farmers revived old methods of producing food. Black butter nights, or sethée d'nier beurre, proved to be the most popular.

Looking at the list of ingredients required, most cooks would have difficulty guessing just what the end product would be. The farmers would prepare the barn, in which there had to be a large fireplace, find the various utensils required, and also obtain the necessary items. Twenty gallons of rough unfermented cider, 22 cwt of sweet apples, 1 cwt of Bramleys, 22 lemons, eight sticks of liquorice, 28 lbs of white sugar, 1 lb of cinnamon, ½ lb of nutmeg and 1 lb of mixed spices. Once the traditional recipe had been carefully followed, these unusual ingredients would produce a thick, dark brown substance much loved by the country folk of the islands.

As apples are the main ingredient, black butter nights take place at the end of October when the apple harvest comes to a close. Once the crop of apples has been picked, the next task, usually performed by the women of the farm, is to peel, core and slice the apples, then store them in terrines or earthenware jars. This operation usually takes place during the few days prior to the evening the butter will be made.

When the allotted day arrives, farmhands will be sent to chop enough wood to keep the open fire going for 24 hours. In the early evening, when the normal day's duties have been completed, everyone involved gathers in the barn. Food and drink in plentiful supply and music — in olden days self-produced, but today coming from a radio or record player — quickly brings out the party spirit.

The first task is to grease the 'bachin' or brass basin with 2 lbs of lard. Then the cider is poured into the bachin which has been placed on a 'trivet' or tripod over the fire. Superstitious farmers add a sprig of hawthorn to the cider in the belief that it will ward off the unwelcome attention of any witches. This is then left for a few hours until the cider has been reduced to half its measure. It is interesting to note that, at this point, if the steam rising from the cider could be caught, passed through a series of pipes and then suddenly cooled, the ensuing liquid would be the apple brandy enjoyed in the north of France called Calvados.

Once the cider is ready, the apples, 28 lbs at a time, are placed into the bachin. From the moment the first apples enter the cider, the mixture has to be continuously stirred. An implement resembling a long-handled hoe called a 'rabot' is used for this long laborious task. A steady backward and forward movement across the bachin has to be maintained to prevent the butter sticking to the sides of the brass vessel and burning. A nail is used to make a mark in the stone or wood above the fireplace to keep tally of the number of loads of apples going into the bachin.

The sweet apples are always used first as they have more juice and water content than the Bramleys. Recipes vary from district to district but most agree on the liquorice being added at this stage to give the colouring. Initially only one man is needed to stir the mixture whilst the remainder of the gathering will be enjoying the party until it is their turn with the rabot. Once the apples are dissolved, another 28 lbs is added until all the sweet apples have been used. It is now time to add the Bramleys and the sugar. The mixture soon thickens as the sugar joins the apples in the bachin which now needs two men to manhandle the rabot in the necessary steady motion. With the increasing thickening of the butter only 14 lbs of apples are added each time. The different spices are then mixed in, and approximately one hour before completion, the grated rind and juice of the lemons.

When the mixture has been tested and pronounced ready, four men, using sacking as webbing, lift the bachin off the fire and place it on the floor of the barn. The women now have the task of filling jam jars with the hot butter. A great deal of noise is made during this part of the operation as each jar has to be banged down on the table to expel any air trapped in the butter. A paper cover, held on with an elastic band, seals the top of the jar.

Twenty-four hours of constant stirring has produced a fairly thick dark brown butter filling about 400 jars from the amount of ingredients used.

This age old custom of black butter making is now kept alive by the Jersey Young Farmers Club purely for charity. The only other place in the world to use this traditional recipe is Pennsylvania in North America. Early emigrants from Jersey to America, hence the area being known as New Jersey, took the custom with them. It spread down to Pennsylvania where it is still made today. Known there as Apple Butter it follows the same recipe and is accompanied by the equivalent festive spirit, keeping alive the customs and traditions of our fore-fathers on both sides of the Atlantic.

THE XIIIth PERQUAGE

'SANCTUARY, SANCTUARY'. These words were made famous by Victor Hugo's hunchback of Notre Dame. In Jersey, before the Reformation, Sanctuary was granted to criminals who took refuge in any of the twelve parish churches. After giving away all his possessions, and in the presence of a Judge and Jurat of the court, he would foreswear to leave the Island. He could then use the Perquage walk which led from each parish church to the sea, and clad only in a white garment, he would depend upon his family to provide a boat to take him to the nearby coast of France.

In 1168, Robert de Torigni, Abbot of the Monastery of Mont St Michel, was given the small Chapel of St Mary, which was situated on the edge of St Ouen's Manor, by Philippe de Carteret, the Seigneur. He formed a Priory of monks from Mont St Michel and changed the name to the Chapel of St Mary de la Wik and was granted a private Perquage to the bay of Grève de Lecq. This was later known as the Chapel of Ste Marie de Lecq before being demolished and fading from the history books.

Perquage walks ceased to exist on March 30th, 1663, by order of King Charles II, who gave the land to Sir Edward de Carteret, Viscount of Jersey.

The gift passed through the Royal Court on July 18th, 1663 when Sir Edward sold the land to the farmers whose fields bordered the Perquages. A few sections of Perquage can still be found, tracing the last walk of many Islanders on their native soil before finding sanctuary in France.

SEAWEED - THE USEFUL FRUIT

TO the majority of people lazing on the beach, seaweed is a nuisance. When rotting it smells, and small flies seem to live in their thousands amongst its tentacles. But nothing in this world is without a use. Many people from all over the world and in different walks of life have found seaweed to be most useful.

The most popular and best known use of seaweed comes in the agricultural field. Farmers have gathered forms of seaweed for many generations. Anywhere that farmland borders the coast, crops are fertilised with the fruits of the sea. Nowhere more so than in the Channel Islands. In the law courts of Jersey as far back as 1600, laws were passed concerning the cutting and gathering of vraic — the local name for seaweed — to ensure that all farmers had equal rights to use this free manure on their fields. After a high tide or a storm, dozens of farmers would descend onto the beach with their horse and carts and gather in the vraic. Stacks were made on the farms and then the manure would be spread over the fields and ploughed in. When the vraic was used on grass it would be allowed to rest on top and slowly rot.

In the west of the Island, which is washed by the rollers of the Atlantic Ocean, a deep water vraic known as Laminariae, noted for its broad leaves, is found. Also species called Dulse — Tangle — Sea Thong — are much sought after as they have a high water content and so make better manure.

In the east, where shallow waters separate Jersey from the nearby coast of France, prevail the vraics known as Channelled. Amongst these the names of

Knotted — Toothed — Bladder Wracks — are most common. Vraic can be gathered off the beaches any day of the year except a Sunday, whilst the cutting of vraic from the rocks is restricted by the law of 1894 to between February 1st and March 30th, once again except on Sundays. In olden days the farmers had a special bun they used to take with them to eat during a break in their toils. These became known as Vraic buns.

Apart from helping to cultivate the land, seaweed is also used as a food. In North Devon and South Wales seaweeds called Porphyra Laciniata and Vulgaris are gathered off the beaches in early spring, stewed many times, then fried or made into a form of bread called Laver. Once the unappetising sight of this meal has been overcome, Laver is found to be an extremely pleasant and nutritious food. In Ireland it is called Slake and is served with pepper, vinegar and butter. It can also be preserved indefinitely in jars.

In the Orkney Islands many locals prospered by harvesting Kelp. It would be gathered in the summer then left to dry. At the end of the season it was burnt and turned into carbonate of lime to be used in the manufacture of soap and glass. In the early 1920s new methods of producing the carbonate of lime were discovered and the farmers of the Orkney's lost much of their lucrative business.

Irish Moss or Carrageen is obtained from the seaweed known as Chondrus Crispus and Chondrus Mamillosus. It is used in the making of soup and blancmange as well as wallpaper size. During the last war the people of the Channel Islands used this particular seaweed as a substitute for jelly.

Seaweed is also found as a base in many medicines, one such example is Iodine. Naturalists buy seaweed capsules proclaiming to be able to cure all manner of illnesses including Arthritis, Rheumatism, Cramp, Depression, Worry, Fatigue, Split nails, Premature sterility, Psoriasis, Anaemia and nervous disorders. Pioneers in this field are the Norwegians who have discovered that in the types of seaweed known as Ascophyllum Nodosum and Laminaria Digitata, there are a great deal of vitamins A, B, C, D and E. In fact the easy answer to good health seems to be to eat seaweed.

Apart from these uses, various other countries have found a way of making seaweed work for them. The French used it as wadding for their cannons and also in the building of houses as a lining for roofs and walls because they found it was a slow conductor of both heat and cold. Denmark collected seaweed for packing and for the stuffing of bedding and cushions, whilst the Chinese use Ceylon Moss for making glue and varnish. Bavaria would not be outdone and instead of Isinglass, they used seaweed for clarifying their beer. It has also been made into rope and knife handles by natives of the South Sea Islands.

The next time you are on the beach and the sea has thrown forth some of its fruits, remember, everything is valuable in some way or form and seaweed is far more than just a nuisance to sunbathers and swimmers.

THE CLAMEUR DE HARO

"Haro, Haro, Haro, a l'aide mon Prince, on me fait tort."

THIS medieval cry for help from Prince Rollo can still be heard today throughout the Channel Islands and the nearby Duchy of Normandy. The cry will be heeded by the law courts and is the strongest form of defence the ordinary citizen has against a person who would do wrong to his neighbour's property.

Prince Rollo came from Denmark in 912 AD and besieged Paris with his vast army. The French king, Charles the Simple, decided to give part of France to Rollo if he would leave Paris alone. Hence the Duchy of Normandy was founded and Rollo became its first Duke.

He was a harsh but just man, making many laws about the rights of the common man. The Clameur de Haro covered the rights of a man's property. When Rollo died in 917 AD his son William took over the Duchy. Having the same warlike qualities as his father, William invaded the neighbouring region of Brittany and brought the area under his command in the year 933 AD, so incorporating the Channel Islands into his kingdom. With this corporation the islands also received a new set of laws known as the Grand Coutumier de Normandie. The Clameur de Haro is one of the few remaining laws from this period.

To incite the Clameur a man would have to find two witnesses, who must have their heads uncovered, then with a witness standing on either side, he would go down on one knee and recite the Clameur.

Haro is an abbreviation of Ahrou which was the name Duke Rollo was known by. The remainder means: 'Help me my Prince, I am being wronged.'

Recent cases include a man who saw his neighbour about to chop down a tree which was partly on his property. He raised the Clameur and the aggressor was immediately forced to stop. If the man had used any other methods, i.e. call the police or go through the usual legal procedure, the tree would probably have been felled before the wheels of justice could have been put into motion.

On May 4th, 1974, Mrs A. Touzel called the Prince to her aid when she found a man lifting potatoes he had unwittingly planted in her mother's côtil. Even though the Royal Court agreed there had been a genuine mistake over the field's boundaries, the man was fined £1 with £5 costs.

If the Clameur is raised without justification the person will be taken to court and fined for improper use of the law. Such was the case in August of 1972, when incorrect raising of the Clameur by Mrs E. Bailhache resulted in a fine of £50 by the court.

The most unusual case involving the raising of the Clameur was at the funeral of William the Conqueror. His coffin was being lowered into a plot of ground owned by one Anselm Fitzarthur, who raised the Clameur thereby stopping the burial. William's son had to bargain with Anselm until a price had been agreed and paid in full, and only then could the funeral continue.

The Clameur de Haro is still as powerful today as it was in 912 AD. Most of Prince Rollo's laws have long been struck from the law books, but the rights of the common man to protect his property still remain, by calling for help from his Prince.

THE PICKET HOUSES

'TURN out the guard and salute.' This order would have been given by the sergeant in charge of the guards stationed at the Picket House each time the St Helier Battalion left town to go on an exercise. The same salute would have been given to the battalion stationed at Elizabeth Castle as they passed the Picket House built near West Park slip.

The first mention of any form of military building at West Park can be found in a contract dated August 15th, 1751. Before Charles Lemprière, Seigneur of Rozel and Lieutenant to the Bailiff of Jersey, sitting with Jurats Jean Le Haroy and Jean Dumaresq, a plot of land was offered, free of charge, to the Crown. The offer came from Charles Bandinel, Seigneur of the Fief de Mèlèches, to Lieutenant-General Jean Huske, Governor of Jersey. This plot of land, measuring 198 feet (9 perches) was situated in front of Elizabeth Castle with the point of the highest tide in March forming the southern boundary. Four boundary stones marked out the extremities of the area, one in each corner, and the barracks were constructed in the centre of the plot and were known as Bridge Foot Barracks.

These barracks were demolished at some later date because there is no mention of them on the plans, dated March 25th, 1865, for the construction of a slipway and a sea wall, eastwards from West Park. After the completion of these drawings, a pencilled rectangle was added near the top of the slip to depict the future position of a Picket House. Therefore the Picket, or Guard House was built sometime during 1865 and 1868 when a further drawing, dated August 20th, 1868, for the construction of the sea wall west of West Park slip shows the Picket House as a finished building. Also a newspaper article of February 3rd, 1869, reports how the newly built Picket House at West Park was damaged by a storm.

The guards stationed at the Picket House would act as an outpost for the battalion housed at Elizabeth Castle. When the soldiers from the castle were off duty, many would follow the causeway, either on foot at low tide, or by using the available rowing boat service, to get to the various inns of the town

The Picket House at West Park.

to relieve their thirst. Any soldier missing the boat back or who turned up at West Park the worse for drink would be forced to spend the night in the Picket House before reporting back to the castle the following morning to receive his punishment.

West Park beach had neat rows of changing huts known as bathing machines stationed close to the sea wall. These were directly below the Picket House, therefore during the summer months it is doubtful whether the guards kept their eyes fixed to the front!

Each November 5th, many bonfires were built on West Park beach and a story is told of one group of youngsters who built an oversize bonfire too close to the Picket House and the guards were called out at the double, armed with buckets of water, to quell the blaze before they became victims of Guy Fawkes night.

The face of West Park could have been changed considerably if a 1922 plan had been put into operation. This consisted of a bridge from the slip to Elizabeth Castle high enough for the crossing to be made on foot regardless of the state of the tide.

Another landmark at West Park which has long disappeared is the boathouse which housed the lifeboat. This building lasted from 1884 until 1895 when it was moved to La Folie slip. The lifeboat at that time was called *Mary and Victoria* and had been supplied by the RNLI. An 1895 plan of the area, drawn up to show the railway and station, which was alongside the Picket House, shows the lifeboat house to be roughly where the statue of Queen Victoria stands today.

The Picket House in the Royal Square came to be through an Act of the States on November 5th, 1802. This followed a suggestion on October 16th, that a plot of land be given to the Crown in order to build a guard house in the middle of town enabling a small force of soldiers to aid the Honorary Police in times of trouble. At that time there was no paid police force in Jersey. A plot situated at the end of the old meat market was found for this building, most of the market having already been sold off. The States decided to include a clause into the act which would make the plot public property again if the Crown did not build a guard house on it.

The Picket House was built and the two-storied building housed the guards posted from the St Helier Battalion at Fort Regent. The Crown continued to use the Picket House until 1834 when, due to the inconvenience of the siting of the building, the property was handed over to the Constable of St Helier, Peter Perrot. It was then used by the police as a lock-up for troublemakers, until the Crown found another use for it. The Paymaster of the garrison decided the building would make an ideal office for paying out pensions to retired soldiers, therefore the Picket House reverted back to the Crown. The Paymaster used the building for an undetermined period of time after which it was vacated. Mr Henry Luce Manual, Registrar of Births, Marriages and Deaths, found the office to his liking and moved in until the war department decided to reclaim it.

The Picket House in the Royal Square.

Mr Manual was forced to vacate the building on January 23rd, 1872 after the Defence Committee demanded a rental of £28 per annum, a sum far above that which he could afford. Numerous letters then changed hands from January 24th until May 5th, 1887, between Major-General Henry Wray the Lieutenant-Governor, Sir George Bertram the Bailiff and Mr W. Bertram

Godfray the States Greffier. These letters referred to whether or not the Crown had the right to take back the Picket House or whether by not occupying it for so long they had relinquished their rights to the property. After these arguments had been settled the Crown continued to use the Picket House, installing a married soldier as caretaker.

Finally the Picket House was sold back to the States in 1934 for the sum of £400. After the German occupation, the States, having no use for the building, decided to let the property to the National Provincial Bank. This was a 99 year lease in which the bank had to make a one-off payment of £500 for passing contract and then one shilling per annum payable on March 25th each year until the lease runs out in 2046. In the lease the bank has the right to demolish the building and rebuild it as long as it is not taller than the remainder of the bank. There is a sundial on one wall of the building which has to remain. If the property were to be demolished, it would have to be incorporated into the new building. The States did not have to provide the bank with water and before the bank could sublet, they would have to receive written permission from the States. After the National Provincial Bank's merger with the Westminster Bank it was decided to lease the building to the Roy West Trust Corporation and the necessary States approval was granted.

The Picket Houses were originally guard houses for the English troops stationed in Jersey to help protect our shores from unwanted visitors. Today both sites are used to welcome visitors to our Island. The Royal Square house is used for Jersey's vast involvement in the world finance market, whilst the old Picket House at West Park, after ending its days as a public toilet, was finally demolished to make way for a café, catering for our tourist industry. Let us hope these welcome visitors continue to come and use these two sites and that we never have to revert back to having guard houses close to our beaches and in the middle of town.

GREEN ISLAND

GREEN ISLAND, or more correctly La Motte, can be found in the bay of St Clement, on the south coast of Jersey. A small rocky outcrop, partly covered with grass — hence the new name of Green Island — it lies a few hundred yards from the beachhead and was certainly once connected to the mainland of Jersey. At low tide the island has a secluded bay favoured by bathers and underwater fishermen. At high tide the island becomes cut off from the shore and the currents can become dangerous.

In 1911, a high tide uncovered a section of stones that interested local historians from the Société Jersiaise. It had long been believed the island had held some other use in the past and the discovery of the stones confirmed in many minds that here was part of a prehistoric grave. On October 12th, 1911, work commenced on excavating the island and on the second day a sepulchral chamber, consisting of two graves, which over the years had been lost beneath the rubble and sand, was uncovered under the clay.

The graves were joined end to end and were approximately 6ft long by 16 inches wide. In the eastern grave a smaller tomb had been constructed about 30 inches long by 9 inches wide, and 12 inches deep. Various bones were discovered along with shells and pieces of pottery. It was thought this was a family grave where a man and woman had been buried with their child. Work continued at a faster rate as winter was drawing in and the high tides could damage or wash away the now open graves.

On October 16th another grave was discovered, similar to the first, only in the eastern section of this grave a skull in excellent condition was found. With the skull were two small axe-shaped implements. Excitement was now rife and more helpers were brought from the Société to dig before the high tides came.

Further graves were uncovered during the next few days with thigh bones and parts of skulls being unearthed. Also amongst the rubble, bones and teeth of various animals such as deer, ox and pig were found. The human skulls were of the variety known as Dolichocephalic, dating back to the New Stone Age race of narrow headed people.

The Société decided to remove the graves and everything that had been found to the safety of the museum. The secrets of Green Island are now on display for all to see — another tiny glimpse of our past and our ancestors preserved for future generations.

THE JERSEY LILY

EMILIE CHARLOTTE LE BRETON was born on October 13th, 1853 at the Old Rectory in St Saviour, Jersey. From a family of seven children she was the only daughter of the Very Rev. William Corbet Le Breton MA, Dean of Jersey, and Emilie Davis Martin. Growing up with six brothers, five of whom were older than her, she became something of a tomboy, learning to play football and cricket. She also adored swimming, rock climbing and horse riding, in all of which she became highly competent. The family had nicknamed her 'Lillie', due to her exceptionally white skin, and she adopted this as her own because of her strong dislike of her given Christian names.

The Old Rectory at St Saviour, birthplace of Lillie Langtry.

As a child, Lillie was always in trouble. The Le Breton children were forever up to some prank or other and a long line of complainants could usually be seen outside the Rectory door. Collecting door knockers, tarring and feathering the statue in the Royal Square, and playing at ghosts during the early evening in the nearby cemetery, complete with white sheets and stilts, were all part of Lillie's repertoire. Madame Bisson, her nanny, most certainly had her hands full. One method she discovered of keeping Lillie out of trouble was by developing her art as a story teller. Lillie would sit for hours listening to the white haired old Frenchwoman telling stories of Jersey's past, through which Lillie learnt how to trace her ancestors back to a Le Breton who had fought alongside William the Conqueror at the Battle of Hastings.

At the age of 13, Lillie developed a taste for spiritualism, and spent many hours round a small table watching the glass spell out messages. In fact she convinced herself she was a medium and her interest in fortune tellers and spiritualists continued throughout her life.

In her early teens Lillie was allowed to attend social functions with her parents, and soon became popular among the locals. Even at this early age her beauty was apparent and her body, through constant exercise, was developing ahead of her years. Lieutenant Charles Spencer Longly, aged 23, son of the Archbishop of Canterbury, whose regiment was stationed in the Island, was the first man to be beguiled by her looks. He presented himself to the Dean to ask for Lillie's hand only to be informed of her true age. Stunned by the news, he immediately requested a posting back to England.

When she was 16, Lillie's mother took her to London in an attempt to complete her education, thus enabling her to mix with society. The Dean of Jersey was well known and they received many invitations to dinner parties. The visit proved a disaster. Lillie couldn't dance, her clothes were not of the latest fashion, and the quantity of knives, forks and spoons on the lavish meal tables bewildered her. Lillie returned to Jersey disillusioned with high society and disappointed at her ability to cope with its problems. She returned to her outdoor activities, losing herself in a life of swimming, rock climbing and horse riding.

As she matured, Lillie became disgruntled with her way of life, yearning to return to London where she felt she was ready to take her rightful place in society. The marriage of a good friend brought a rich Irish yachtsman, Edward Langtry, to the Island. He sailed into St Helier harbour in his ship *The Red Gauntlet* and threw a party for the newly weds at the local yacht club. Edward became captivated with Lillie's beauty and the couple became constant companions. Although not really in love with Edward, Lillie could see her ideal opportunity to escape the confines of the Island. She consented to his proposal and the couple were married, by Lillie's father, in St Saviour's church in March 1874.

They sailed off on their honeymoon in *The Red Gauntlet*, making their home at Edward's house in Southampton called *Cliffe Lodge*. Here the couple spent the first year of their marriage, Edward happy to be close to his yacht and the fishing grounds, Lillie discontented with the life of a country housewife. There were little or no social events in Southampton and managing a large house was not one of her better accomplishments. Eventually the day-to-day running of affairs was left to the butler and being thoroughly bored with her lot, her health deteriorated. At last the family doctor, probably under the influence of Lillie's beauty and with a few subtle hints from his patient, decided it would benefit her health if the couple moved to London. Edward finally succumbed and on their first wedding anniversary the house in Southampton was sold and they moved into the bright social life of London.

Edward Langtry.

Lillie found life in London, as an unknown, equally as boring as life in Southampton. Edward detested the city and longed for the open water and his fishing trips. The premature death of her brother Reggie, brought Lillie back to Jersey where she remained with her parents for several weeks. In an attempt to cheer up their daughter, they commissioned Jersey's only dressmaker of note, Madame Nicholle, to make Lillie a new dress. The plain black dress did not impress Lillie but was to have a great bearing on her future success in London.

Moving back to the city, the couple continued their dismal existence. Even though they socialised at public functions no private invitations were forthcoming. In April 1876 everything suddenly changed. Edward and Lillie attended the opening of the Royal Aquarium in Westminster and a chance meeting with Lord and Lady Ranelagh, who had paid several visits to the Rectory in Jersey, resulted in an invitation to a drinks party. Amongst the lavishly dressed ladies, glittering with jewels, Lillie stood out. With no jewellery, her plain black dress and her hair tied up in a bun, she showed off her exceptional beauty to the extent that everyone in the room was soon enquiring about the solitary stranger in the corner. Lillie wasn't alone for long. Soon the gentlemen present formed a circle around her, asking all manner of questions. Invitations poured through the Langtry's letter box and Lillie became the centre of attention at many dinner parties.

Famous painters clamoured for a sitting but Lillie chose Millais — mainly because he came from Jersey — to be the first to capture her on canvas. She wore the now famous black dress for the sitting and Millais, thinking something else was required to break the colour, had a lily called 'Nerine Sarniensis' brought over especially from Jersey. The crimson lily gave the finishing touch to his masterpiece, which is still considered to be the finest painting of Lillie. Millais chose the title 'A Jersey Lily', a name which remained with her for the rest of her life.

Oscar Wilde was also captivated by her beauty and composed a special poem called *The New Helen*'. He presented her with a white vellum bound copy inscribed: 'To Helen, formerly of Troy, now of London'.

At one dinner party, Lillie was escorted to the dinner table by a distinguished looking American, where she unwittingly shocked everyone present by asking him what he had done since the American civil war. General Ulysses Simpson Grant smiled as he explained he had just finished his second term as President of the United States. He was the first of many Americans to be smitten by the Jersey Lily.

To every function and social event Lillie always wore her famous black dress, no jewellery and her plain hair style. For over a year no-one had ever seen her in anything different until, after lending the dress to a friend, it was returned with the seams split. Lillie decided on a complete contrast and attended her next outing in white velvet. It was at this time that she first encountered the Prince of Wales.

Albert Edward, eldest son of Queen Victoria, was a great lover of beautiful women. Although married and a father of five children he had a name in society for having a roving eye. Bets were laid as to the outcome of the first confrontation between the Prince and the famous Lillie Langtry who had spurned so many would-be lovers. The meeting was at the home of Sir Allen Young, famous for his lobster curry of which the Prince was particularly fond.

It proved to be an anti-climax because the Prince only exchanged a few pleasantries with everyone, including Lillie, then left the party.

Lillie didn't believe in conforming to fashion. She liked to create the fashion, and with clothes designed for comfort rather than show, she led the field. The ladies of society waited to see how 'The Lily' would dress, then followed suit. Her hairstyle, plain and simple, was also copied and all the top dressmakers and hairstylists of the day would attend to Lillie's requirements without the usual high charges. In doing so they could advertise themselves 'By Appointment to Lillie Langtry' and so multiply their business.

'A Jersey Lily' by Millais. *The Prince of Wales.*

The Prince of Wales had by now fallen for the beauty of the Jersey Lily. Several other party engagements, at which he was present, had left him completely captivated by Mrs Langtry. Their relationship was the talk of the world press. They were seen everywhere together. Race meetings, riding in the park, dinner parties. To be certain of the Prince attending any party, all the hostess had to do was invite Lillie Langtry.

In the spring of 1880, Lillie left London for a short holiday away from her husband, who had virtually become an alcoholic. He went on one of his many fishing trips whilst Lillie made it known she was going to visit her parents in Jersey. In fact she only stayed with them for a few days, then went to Paris where she booked into the exclusive Hotel Bristol. The Prince of Wales, travelling incognito, also booked into the same hotel and, by chance, his apartment was on the same floor. The couple were seen at every Parisian night spot, and during the daytime they took in the sights, constantly shadowed by nervous British Embassy officials.

Shortly after, with Edward away on another of his fishing trips, Lillie, to her dismay, found she was pregnant. The couple hadn't slept together for over a year, so Lillie made no mention of it in her letter to Edward asking him for a separation. Lillie also found that both she and her husband had run up considerable debts which neither could afford to settle. The dilemma was overcome by a loan of £2,000 from the Prince's best friend, Sir Allen Young, who had first introduced the couple. Both the Prince and Princess of Wales visited Lillie at her London flat and on the express orders of the Princess, the Royal Household Physician, Francis Laking, constantly attended Lillie. To keep the news from the press and her husband, Lillie went to Jersey to have her baby. Strangely, no record of the birth can be found in any register, but in either March or April of 1881, Lillie gave birth to a daughter, Jeanne Marie Langtry.

Lillie couldn't settle down to being a mother or living in a small Island after her few years in high society, so she found a governess to take care of Jeanne, and moved back to London. Things were now very different for the Jersey Lily. London society had turned their backs on her because of her relationship with the Prince, her financial status and her marriage problems. Lillie, knowing she would have to have some source of income, decided she would like to become an actress. Henrietta Hodson Labouchère came to her aid, not only with acting lessons but with her first part on the stage. On November 19th, 1881 at Twickenham Town Hall, Lillie starred in a one act play lasting just half an hour called *A Fair Encounter*. As the curtains opened to reveal the packed house, Lillie froze and forgot her lines. Mrs Labouchère, who was playing the other part in the play, gave Lillie the necessary prompting and the play was completed to much applause.

Next came a charity performance in aid of the Royal General Theatrical Fund at the Theatre Royal in the Haymarket on December 15th. Lillie played Kate Hardcastle in '*She Stoops to Conquer*' and the Prince and Princess of Wales graced the occasion by sitting in the royal box. The press gave Lillie a good review, saying that although she still showed signs of amateurism, here was a definite star in the making.

Offers flooded in and Lillie soon found herself on the road to success. A tour of the provinces followed, with '*She Stoops to Conquer*' playing to packed houses. Whilst in Edinburgh, one member of the audience, Henry E. Abbey from New York, was so taken by Lillie's beauty and performance as an actress that he offered her a season in America. The financial position was being settled when Lillie caused a stir in London society by becoming the first woman to endorse a commercial product. She was paid one hundred and thirty two pounds by Pears Soap Ltd, to make the statement that her flawless skin was due to using no soap other than Pears. The fee was determined by Lillie's weight. They paid her pound for pound.

Lillie left Liverpool aboard the *Arizona* on October 14th, 1882, arriving in New York on October 23rd amidst great scenes of revelry and strains of *'God Save The Queen'*. Everywhere she went traffic was brought to a standstill and even Wall Street closed the stock exchange during her visit to the great hall of finance. Henry Le York wrote a special tune in her honour and *The Jersey Lily Waltz* became one of the most popular tunes of the year.

The Park Theatre was the venue for Lillie's first performance in the States and, due to the immense demand for tickets, the boxes and stall seats were auctioned by W. Olliver of the New York Stock Exchange for 20,000 dollars. With only 48 hours to go before the curtain rose, the Park Theatre was burnt to the ground. Henry Abbey would not be put off by an incident he termed as 'a small setback'. He immediately hired the much larger Wallack's Theatre and the show made Lillie a star on both sides of the Atlantic. The critics were not so impressed, and slated her acting but still the crowds flocked in their thousands to every performance.

In order to obtain a divorce, Lillie applied for American citizenship on July 17th, 1887 as the laws pertaining to divorce were easier than in Britain. Soon after this time she ended her marriage to Edward Langtry. She also took a few well chosen lovers including millionaire Fred Gebhard, and a Scotsman called George Baird. The latter was extremely rich but lacked breeding and manners. After finding her dining with a friend in Paris he blackened both her eyes, putting her in hospital for ten days. In an attempt to regain favour he gave her presents of jewellery, horses and finally a magnificent 220ft, 700 ton steamship called *The White Ladye*. Lillie forgave him but their relationship was never the same. Newspapermen, always on the lookout for a story or a joke about the Jersey Lily, renamed the ship *The Black Eye*.

The White Ladye.

When asked how she kept her figure so trim, Lillie answered 'jogging'. No-one knew what she meant until she explained how she would go for a two mile run every morning at the crack of dawn. She was a fitness fanatic but she surprised everyone when she became the first women to be seen smoking in public. Lillie could never stick to protocol. She made up her own rules as she went along and the public at large followed her every move, always trying to keep up with the 'Jersey Lily'.

'Mrs Langtry' by Sir Edward Poynter (courtesy of the Jersey Museum).

A San Francisco newspaperman discovered the details of her American divorce including the fact that Jeanne was her daughter and not her niece, as everyone had been led to believe. Edward Langtry, who also hadn't known about Jeanne, took the news badly, and in the spring of 1897 he was committed to a mental asylum, his brain completely ruined by his constant drinking.

Lillie's love of horses came from her childhood days in Jersey where she was a frequent visitor at the annual Jersey Race Meeting on Gorey Common.

She continued this hobby in later years, choosing fawn and blue as her colours and using the assumed name of Mr Jersey as a horse owner. At one time she had twenty horses in training at the stable of Fred Webb in Exning. Her best horse was Merman who won the Cesarewitch one hour after Edward Langtry died in the asylum. Merman also won the Goodwood Cup, Jockey Club Cup and the Ascot Gold Cup. Later she bought Yentoi and, trained by Fred Darling, he also won the Cesarewitch. Lillie had a favourite horse called Maud Mackintosh. The mare became a great pet even though she never won any major races. After an unsuccessful race at Newmarket, the horse collapsed and died of heart failure and Lillie wept openly in the paddock over the body of her horse.

Constant criticism from the press, combined with the fact that she was now 45 years old and reputed to be worth over two million dollars, caused Lillie to retire from both stage and horse racing. Her name was linked with numerous men until Lillie ended all the speculation by marrying Hugo de Bathe, 19 years her junior, at St Saviour's Church in Jersey during the summer of 1899.

The call of the stage and footlights was too great for Lillie to stay away long. Appearing in the play *The Degenerates* in London, she received rapturous applause and decided to take the play to America. To enable Lillie to travel in comfort, Colonel Mann, inventor of the Mann boudoir railway carriage, designed and built a luxury coach called the Lalee which is Indian for flirt. It was 75ft long and Lillie described it as resembling Cleopatra's barge, with wheels but without the purple sails. The exterior was painted blue with wreaths of golden lilies encircling the name. Brass lilies decorated the outside and the teak platform had been specially brought from India. The interior consisted of a large sleeping compartment which was padded in Nile green silk brocade to resist shock in case of collision, complete with a private adjoining bathroom which had silver fittings. The saloon was spacious and even included a grand piano. There were two guest rooms, a maid's room, pantry, kitchen and sleeping quarters for the staff. Lillie travelled all over the States in the Lalee until it was eventually destroyed by fire.

Lillie bought a 6,500 acre ranch in California in a place called Lake Country, naming it Langtry Farms. Her ranch was open to allcomers and the Indians used it as their hunting grounds, even killing her own branded cattle. Lillie commissioned a Frenchman from Bordeaux to organise her vineyard, and produced a wine with her picture on the bottle. The law of prohibition placed all liquor into bond for a number of years, hence no sales were ever recorded. Disillusioned with the ranch, she sold it at a great loss, one of the few times Lillie didn't make a profit from a business venture.

Back in England Lillie made her only stage appearance in her native Island of Jersey when, on July 9th, 1900, she opened a new theatre called the Opera House with the play *The Degenerates*.

On June 30th, 1902 Jeanne, now a young lady of beauty in her own right, married Sir Ian Malcolm, a leading Tory MP. Breaking all tradition, the bride was given away by her mother. The groom's family wasn't overjoyed with their daughter-in-law's mother and Lillie saw less and less of her daughter, except for the occasional visits Jeanne would pay her whilst her husband was away on parliamentary affairs.

Lillie then took the play *Mrs Deering's Divorce* to America, and on opening night in New York, she shocked the audience by incorporating a new scene into the play where she disrobed down to her underclothes before donning a dressing gown. It was during this tour that Lillie paid her only visit to the town of Langtry in Texas. The town had been founded by Judge Roy Bean, one of her most devout admirers. As Lillie arrived aboard the Lalee, she was greeted by the entire population of Langtry headed by the new judge, W. H. Dodd. He told Lillie that Roy Bean had died just a few months previously, and presented her with the judge's revolver with the inscription: "Presented by W. H. Dodd, of Langtry, Texas, to Mrs Lillie Langtry, in honour of her visit to our town." She was taken on a short tour of Langtry including having a drink at the Jersey Lily Saloon before leaving, laden with many gifts.

During the First World War Lillie played in many charity concerts, raising money to help the wounded on both sides of the Atlantic. She crossed the ocean many times, evading the waiting enemy submarines, to continue the performances.

She became the world's most glamourous grandmother at the age of 51, although her relationship with Jeanne had deteriorated to the point where communication was non-existent. During this period, Lillie wrote her only novel called *All At Sea,* starred in her one attempt at motion pictures with *His Neighbour's Wife,* and broke the bank of Monte Carlo. Life was never dull. Even when she spent the last year of the war in Kentford for safety reasons, she wasn't idle, helping the local girls cultivate vegetables for the war effort.

With the end of the war Lillie decided to retire to Monaco, where towards the end of her life the rift between mother and daughter was finally bridged, enabling Lillie to meet her four grandchildren, three boys and a girl. In the autumn of 1928, when Lillie was 75 years old, she caught bronchitis complicated with pleurisy. Even though she recovered, her condition was weak and in February 1929 she suffered a dose of influenza. She was confined to bed and on February 12th, 1929, the world famous Jersey Lily died.

Her body was brought back to her Island home and buried in St Saviour's cemetery with the rest of her family. A French sculptor captured her image in stone and the bust was placed over her grave as a lasting memorial to the beautiful woman who had won so many hearts, broken most of them, and had always lived life by her own rules, ignoring tradition, ensuring that the world would always remember the name of Lillie Langtry, the Jersey Lily.

GROSNEZ CASTLE

GROSNEZ CASTLE, situated at the most north-westerly point of Jersey, is the mystery castle of the Island. Unlike Gorey or Elizabeth Castles, there is hardly any mention in the history books or old manuscripts about this fortification. It was a roughly-built fort because no master builder was employed, the work being carried out by the people of the surrounding area, between 1328 and 1330, as protection from attacks by the French.

Grosnez was not built to withstand a prolonged siege as there was no water supply inside the castle. Water had to be carried from a spring some 200 yards away before any siege started, and then stored. The fortification was roughly circular in shape, with a perimeter of about 250 yards. On three sides it was defended mainly by sheer cliffs and a low wall. Only on the south side did the castle have any real defences. These consisted of a ditch with a gatehouse and drawbridge towering above it. On each side of the portcullis and gatehouse was a two-storey tower or bastion with 6ft thick walls and arrow slits for the archers to fire down on the foe beneath. The whole building was covered with a battlement roof.

Inside the castle there were no secondary walls, so once an enemy had penetrated the outer defences, victory was virtually certain. The only buildings inside were a few small houses or shelters, the foundations of which can still be seen. Grosnez is known to have been captured in 1468 and destroyed sometime between then and 1540, when it was left in ruins.

Most of the stone used in its construction came from the Mont Mado area of St John, and after the castle's destruction local inhabitants used some of the stone for their houses and walls around their fields. By the position of the stones it is certain the castle was destroyed and not simply left to crumble with age.

An archway and low walls are all that remain of Grosnez Castle, a silent reminder of a past era whose history has been mostly lost with the passing of time.

THE HOUSE OF CORRECTION

MONT ORGUEIL CASTLE at Gorey provided the Island of Jersey with its only prison from the end of the 15th century until the middle of the 17th century. At least one tower of the castle, known as the Prison Busgros or the Prison Criminall, was used, not only for persons convicted by the local civil authorities but for political prisoners banished from the mainland.

Local prisoners, after being convicted by the courts, were taken to the Royal Square, which in those days was used as the market place. There they would be put into iron cages to await their removal to Mont Orgueil by the Hallebardiers, or prison guards, who were recruited from the parishes of St Martin, Grouville and St Saviour. This iron cage, or temporary prison, was dismantled on March 2nd, 1697.

On March 5th, 1646, Sir George Carteret gave a house in the Fief du Prieur de L'Islet, near Charing Cross, to the States of Jersey as the first house of correction. Although small, this house was used for civil prisoners until the States decided to build a new prison. Money was raised for this project by taxing all French vessels using the harbour of St Helier at the rate of five shillings per ton. In March 1684 the land was purchased and on January 20th, 1686, the States authorised the Bailiff, Sir Peter de Carteret, to draw up the necessary plans for the building of a new house of correction with a larger capacity than the existing one.

In every parish, the States proclaimed that all Constables and their officers apprehend, in their respective parishes, the following persons:

1. All swearers and blasphemers of God's Holy Name.
2. Profaners of the Sabbath whether by playing games or frequenting taverns or those who neglected to come to divine service and listen to the sermons.
3. Children rebellious towards their parents.
4. Indentured servants who quitted their employment before their period of indenture had expired.
5. Those persons, male or female, who have neither house nor a family, but who are capable of ploughing the ground, or those who are compelled to stay indoors and those who refuse to let themselves be hired out at reasonable wages.
6. All men capable of work if they be found knitting with women and girls in public places other than in the house where they live.
7. All beggars not possessing a licence to do so from either the Rector or the Constable and his Principals, it being understood that no-one will be licensed unless he is incapable of working for a living.
8. All Islanders and disparagers of persons holding esteem and propagators of false rumours.

9. Those persons who have a family and threaten to leave it or those who do not wish to work for the upkeep of their family.
10. All taverners and bakers who have been forbidden to carry on their profession and who continue notwithstanding.

With such strict laws, gross overcrowding of the cells was inevitable and work commenced in 1688 at the site in Charing Cross which was the only entrance into the town of St Helier from the west of the Island. The new house of correction was built over the road, giving the impression of a city gate and all traffic had to pass through the archway on their way into or out of town. Prisoners were first kept there in 1693 although the building wasn't completed until 1699.

Built between Rue de Derrière (King Street) and Grande Rue (Broad Street) the prison was a large two storied building of Jersey granite with underground dungeons known as Les Basses Fosses, meaning Deep Trenches. On the ground floor were two large dungeons for criminals under sentence of death — public hanging took place on Gallows Hill at Westmount — whilst above was the room for common criminals, which had a stone floor, and another for debtors with a wooden floor. Three large closets were provided for prisoners condemned to solitary confinement.

A stream flowed outside the walls on the townside of the prison and as the windows of the lower dungeons, which were too small to allow much light to filter through, were level with the ground, the cells were damp and infested with rats. The debtors upstairs faired slightly better as their cells were not so damp, although the meagre amount of food provided for the prisoners forced them to beg from passers-by. This they would do by lowering small bags, attached to pieces of string out of the windows, in the hope that some kindly person would give either bread, money or tobacco.

The noise of heavy carts passing through the arch echoed through the lower dungeons and there were rumours of evil spirits in the form of large serpents, who when woken up by the noise, would enter Les Basses Fosses and devour the prisoners.

On the right hand side of the prison was the jailer's quarters, complete with kitchen and storeroom. Several closets were also above his rooms where debtors could be housed when the main cells were overcrowded. From September 11th, 1802 until the prison ceased to operate on March 5th, 1814, the head gaoler was Mr Thomas Labey, who lived for his 11½ years of service in his quarters at the prison.

At the rear of the prison was a small garden approximately four perches in size where vegetables were grown for the prisoners. No space had been provided for exercise so the criminals would spend their sentence confined to their cramped cells, with the exception of market days when they would be placed in the pillory situated in the market place, to receive the scorn of the locals. This form of punishment continued until the pillory was last occupied on November 19th, 1836.

The law was exceedingly harsh, as one David Brouard, whose crime has been lost with the passing of time, found out on June 23rd, 1787. He was sentenced to be whipped from the Court House to the prison. There he had his right ear cut off and nailed to the prison door.

By 1749 the prison was in such a bad state of repair, that the States were forced to consider building a new, and much larger prison. Work commenced in 1811 on the site in Newgate Street and was finished in 1814. Demolition of the old prison was started on February 1st, 1811, even though prisoners were still being housed in the lower dungeons.

The site of the old house of correction at Charing Cross is now occupied by the offices of Rumsey and Rumsey, and although the underground dungeons remain, they have been cemented over. Les Basses Fosses no longer echo to the screams of criminals tied to the whipping straps, which were still in the walls when workmen laid the new floor above. It can only be hoped, for the sake of the employees of the new owners, that the legendary serpents have also moved to pastures new.

A CEMETERY FOR ANIMALS

"Here rest the remains of our friends below,
Blest with more sense than half the folk we know,
Fond of their ease, and to no parties prone,
They damn'd no sect, but calmly gnawed their bone,
Performed their functions well in every act,
Blush Christians, if you can, and copy that,
There's an empty place in our hearts today,
For our best pal has gone away."

THESE are the words of Mrs E. A. Bellis who, in 1928, founded the Jersey Animal Cemetery, allowing owners to bury their pets in peaceful surroundings, as a tribute to the love and affection they had received during the animal's life. Though most animals laid to rest are either dogs or cats, the many visitors who wander around the well-kept graves can find headstones in memory of two horses, a monkey, a goat, numerous rabbits, hamsters and white mice.

In the case of the horses, Judy aged 27 and Dolly aged 36, only headstones were permitted, as the bodies would have taken up too much space. The stones were placed in the cemetery, not by the owner, but by a gentleman who for many years regularly hired a limousine and, armed with carrots and sugar, visited the field where the horses grazed.

Many of the headstones, which must not stand more than 2ft high, are beautifully inscribed. One animal lover wrote: "It broke our hearts to lose you, but you did not go alone, part of us went with you, the day God called you home." Whilst another grieving owner had the words: "Goodnight little one, we will meet again in the morning" inscribed on the headstone.

One dog was buried surrounded by his toys, with a cross around his neck and flowers in his paws. Many were wrapped in their favourite blankets, whilst two dogs shipped over from Blackpool by their owner, who had strong Jersey connections, were found to have lead-lined coffins.

Police dogs, guide dogs, hotel and public house pets lie side by side. The dog no longer chases the cat, they rest together, remembered by the loved ones they left behind. One boxer called 'Tina' who died in 1971, has a plant placed against her tombstone every year on the anniversary of her death, whilst a black and white terrier has his picture attached to his gravestone.

'Jersey Nell' has a special place in the cemetery. She died on November 17th, 1936 and was one of the best known dogs in Jersey because she regularly collected for charity in a local store. She raised over £400 before her death, which in those days was a significant amount.

All animals are now buried in PVC bags as opposed to wooden coffins solely because of subsidence due to decomposure. The cost of transport and burial is £32.00. This includes a fee to cover the cost of maintaining the cemetery to a standard far above that of any graveyard used for human burial. Headstones can cost between £45 and £50, but the cost of burying your pet is much less than that of a cemetery in Essex for example, where a charge of £60 is made for burial alone.

The number of pets laid to rest has risen over the years. When the Jersey Animal Shelter took over the running of the cemetery late into 1957 and started keeping records, they showed that in 1958 only 14 dogs were buried compared with 1983, when 66 dogs and 18 cats were interned.

The man in charge of the shelter and cemetery, Mr A. J. Raffray, conducts funerals on Monday, Wednesday and Friday mornings and visitors are allowed every day between 9.00 a.m. and 4.30 p.m.

This small plot of land, within a stone's throw of beautiful sandy beaches and lush green parks, where many animals are taken for their daily exercise, is a constant, silent reminder that an animal is still a man's best friend. In the words of one owner. "To Jimmy and Charley, our Siamese friends, who gave us their love and devotion for nine years. They died together, March 15th, 1954. Rest in peace."

JERSEY CABBAGE WALKING STICKS

HOW many ways could you use a cabbage? Most people, anywhere in the world, would confine their answers to different ways of cooking the vegetable. In Jersey, the farmers with their "waste not, want not" attitude to life, came up with many different ideas for the cabbages.

Firstly, it must be said we are talking about a special type of cabbage; Brassica oleracae longata (Acephala group), to give it its true Latin name, or more commonly known as Cow Cabbage, Jersey Kale or Long Jacks.

These cabbages have been grown in Brittany and parts of Northern France for hundreds of years and can still be found on a few French farms. In 1827, a total of 36 seeds were sent from La Vendée in France to six different agriculturalists throughout Britain, where the experiment was unsuccessful and the cabbage proved unpopular. Whether Jersey was part of this original experiment is not known. It is possible the seeds had been introduced many years before by Breton farmers; however, by 1836 records show that the giant cabbage was being grown all over the Island.

The giant cabbage originally had many uses. The leaves were used as fodder for the cows, they were also wrapped around dough to produce the well known cabbage loaf. During the summer, men would place a giant leaf inside their hats to keep themselves cool whilst working in the fields, and a warm leaf was also meant to be good for a bad back. The old Jersey recipe for "soupe à choix" consisted of the leaves boiled with potatoes and lard, sometimes with the introduction of meat and red wine.

The stalks were also put to many uses. They made excellent cross rafters beneath the thatch roofs of the farm cottages, bean poles and tomato canes, fuel for the farm kitchen and finally came the unusual idea of producing walking sticks from the long sturdy stalks.

Mr Henry Charles Gee was one of the first to manufacture the walking sticks on a commercial basis. From his shop at 27 Beresford Street, locals and tourists alike bought cabbage walking sticks from the early 1870s until 1928. Between 500 and 600 were sold every year during this period. His daughter Nellie then took over the running of the shop and continued with the trade of cabbage walking sticks even though sales dropped off to about 150 per year during the 1930s.

Mr Gee had certain farmers who would grow the cabbages especially for his walking sticks and he would visit these farms at harvest time to carefully choose which stalks he could turn into his famous walking canes. Not every stalk would produce a good walking stick and Mr Gee had to be extremely selective

The seeds can be planted at any time of the year and it takes eight months before the cabbage is ready for harvest. The tale of planting the seeds when the moon is full during the months of August or September is purely a story for the tourists. The cabbages for the 1986 harvest were planted on a wet day in March and they will be pulled up during late November. As the cabbage grows, the lower leaves are removed to allow the stalks to strengthen. When the cabbage is ready it is pulled up with its roots intact, stacked upside down for four to five weeks, then placed in a loft for up to six months to dry out. During this time the stalk should be turned regularly to avoid rot. When the cabbages are harvested most will have reached at least five to six feet, although cabbages measuring 15 feet are common and some of 20 feet have been recorded.

Three different types of sticks were produced. First the straight walking stick which has always been the most popular. This stick was finished off with a Jersey 1d coin fixed into the mount at the top of the cane; today the coin has been replaced with the Jersey coat of arms. Secondly there was the crook handle stick with its curved handle and lastly the hook handle stick which came out at right angles from the shaft. Mr Gee used to bend the handles by burying the sticks in a furnace filled with sand and boiling the cabbage sticks until the ends could be bent with irons.

All the walking sticks were finished with a strong brass ferrule and steel roundel at the base. Today a rubber ferrule is used. Sandpapering was an important part of the finish to the stick. First rough paper was used, then medium and lastly fine sandpaper for the end finish. Two coats of varnish or clear polyurethane was then applied to give the stick its glossy finish which helps to protect the cane.

The trade in cabbage walking sticks was revived in 1946 by Phil Le Gresley, founder of L'Etacq Woodcrafts. His craftsmen make use of the whole stalk by producing thimbles, fly swats, shoehorns, corkscrews, key rings, shaving brush and razor handles plus ingenious ghost-like creatures from the roots which are sprayed in different colours and given large round eyes. Nothing is wasted and the method used in making the walking canes is the same now as it was a century ago when Mr Gee first started using cabbages as walking sticks.

JANVRIN'S TOMB

THE death of Philippe Valpy dit Janvrin can be attributed in certain aspects to an order of the States of Jersey — an order which forced all vessels arriving in the Island, from certain ports of France, to undergo a period of quarantine before being permitted to land because of an outbreak of the plague in Marseilles and other parts of France.

Philippe Janvrin was the third son of Jacques Valpy dit Janvrin and Marie Le Couteur of St Brelade. He was born in 1677 and at the age of 33, married Elizabeth, daughter of Philippe Orange, in the parish church of St Brelade on September 27th, 1710. The marriage was blessed with five children: Philippe born in 1713, Jacques born in 1715, Jean whose date of birth is not recorded, Elizabeth who died as an infant and another daughter named Elizabeth born in 1718.

Philippe Janvrin was a seaman and he regularly ploughed the oceans in his ship the *Esther* of which he was the master. On September 23rd, 1721, Philippe was sailing his ship from Nantes to Jersey when he was forced to weigh anchor in Belle Croute Bay because of the quarantine order from the States of Jersey.

Although tourists to the Island are often told the story that the ship's crew were infected with the plague, all the written evidence of the time points to the ship being free from infection. Nevertheless, Philippe Janvrin contracted what was described on his tombstone as an ordinary fever and died on the second day of quarantine, whilst at anchor just off Portelet. He was aged 44. Due to the rumours of plague, neither his wife or children dared go to him and his body was not allowed to be brought ashore.

In the middle of Portelet Bay is a small islet know as Ile au Guerdain, named after a family called Le Goupil dit Guerdain who owned all the land surrounding the bay. Permission was given by the Royal Court, with the consent of the Lieutenant-Governor, to bury Philippe Janvrin on the islet. Three seamen from the *Esther* were assigned to row his body from the ship to the islet for burial. The fact that there were seamen alive on board the *Esther* counteracts many reports, that Philippe was the last person to die on board as all his seamen had already been killed by the plague.

Philippe Janvrin's family and friends attended the funeral on September 27th, 1721 by standing on the hillside overlooking Portelet Bay. As the three seamen started lowering the coffin into the grave, they gave a signal to the grieving relatives on the hillside, and the minister, the Rev. Philippe Messervy BA, who was standing next to the widow, read the Service for the Burial of the Dead. Philippe Janvrin's widow instructed that a tombstone be placed over the grave with the inscription: 'Here awaiting a happy resurrection, lies the body of Philippe Janvrin of St Brelade'.

History is also divided as to whether or not his body was later moved to the cemetery of St Brelade. No records can be found in the parish register of any re-burial so it appears his remains are still on the islet.

The tower that stands on the islet of Ile au Guerdain today, has no connection with Philippe Janvrin as it was built 87 years after his death. This tower was constructed, on the instructions of General Don, as part of the fortifications of the Island against possible French raids during the Napoleonic Wars. General Don instigated the building of the tower on March 16th, 1808 and it was fully manned and equipped with cannon by 1811.

The story of Philippe Janvrin is an unfortunate one. If he indeed died of an ordinary fever and not the plague, it was only an order of the States of

Jersey which stopped him from landing and receiving treatment from a doctor, which may have enabled him to live a full life, and his body would not have been laid to rest in unconsecrated ground on the small rocky islet of Ile au Guerdain.

THE ORMER

ON an extremely low tide our forefathers would gather in their hundreds, follow the receding water and ignoring the cold, wade in up to their waists. The only thought was a feast of . . . *ormers*.

This would have been the scene years ago in the Channel Islands when the ormer was in plentiful supply. Today it is dozens instead of hundreds who brave the cold in search of the elusive ormer. Whether it is due to overfishing, divers with aqualungs strapped to their backs or the decreasing temperatures of the past few years, one thing is certain, there just aren't enough ormers to go round. The days when a man could fill his *pannier-a-cou* or wicker-work basket to the brim have gone. The ormers have packed their bags and moved to another shoreline.

The Channel Islands ormer is just one of 75 species. Found all over the world. They are considered a delicacy in America, Australia, New Zealand, Japan and China. The type of ormer found in local waters has its centre in the Mediterranean. From there it spreads south to Guinea after which it becomes too hot, and north to the Channel Islands and nearby coast of France after which the temperature is too cold. Therefore the Channel Islands are right on the edge of the ormers' limits and a few bad summers followed by colder than usual winters could have been enough to make the ormer move further south in search of warmer waters.

The ormer has been around for thousands of years. It was mentioned by Aristotle in the 4th Century BC when it was known as the 'Wild Limpet'. Other names have been Abalone, Mutton Fish and Sea Ear, whilst the humble ormer has the illustrious Latin name of *Haliotis Tuberculata*.

The ormer is a hermaphrodite—having both male and female sex organs—and they are vegetarians, living off the kelp and other forms of algae which grow around our rocky coastline. Their enemies include the octopus, starfish, oystercatchers who can break through the strong shell with just one jab of their beaks, and of course—man.

In 1673, a story published in *News From The Channel* told how the ormer had become a good source of food in the islands and how the shells were used as decoration on many houses and walls. The mother of pearl finish inside the ormer shell has also been used in necklaces and other forms of jewellery, whilst inside some shells, pearls have been discovered. In 1959 an ormer found off Jersey had no less than 18 separate pearls inside. This exhibit can now be found in the local museum.

The ormering season runs from September 1st until April 30th; in fact any month with an 'R' in it means it's permissible to gather ormers. Regardless of which of these months you choose it is only worth following the tide down on a really low tide because only then are the rocks exposed where the ormers can be found. Any person who decides to try their hand at low water fishing for ormers must always obey two simple rules. If you turn over a rock always turn it back again to allow the continued growth of small algae and it is also important to keep an eye on the tide. The speed at which the tide comes in after it has turned is, in some areas, faster than a man can walk.

The shell is as beautiful as the taste of the ormer itself. When cleaned and polished, the shell makes an unusual ashtray or decorative ornament. Close inspection will reveal a series of small holes through which all the ormer's sense organs extrude, excretory matter passes and spawning takes place. It was once thought the ormer made one hole each year so you could tell the age of an ormer by the number of holes in the shell. This has recently been proved incorrect as the ormer grows five such perforations each year and when one is no longer required it can be easily filled in.

Divers almost made the ormer extinct until the practice of aqualung diving for these delicacies was made illegal. The States of Guernsey, in an effort to replenish the beds, are in the process of trying an experiment with five ormer hives in different parts of the Island. The growth of the ormers plus all other important information regarding the welfare and breeding of this species of univalve mollusc are carefully monitored. The experiment commenced in September 1983 and today each hive contains between 800 and 3,000 ormers.

If you are lucky enough to be able to catch or buy some ormers and would like to taste this unusual gastronomic delicacy here are a few ideas on how to cook them.

In all cases remove the ormer from the shell, clean thoroughly, scrubbing the muscular foot to remove the slime and black pigment. Discard the intestines and the small tentacles which contain the eyes, then beat the ormer with a steak mallet or rolling pin. Prick with a fork, then fry both sides until golden brown.

At this stage you could try one of many recipes. Firstly coat in seasoned flour, then place in a casserole dish with half a bottle of dry white wine and cook for at least five hours on a moderate heat.

Another method is to mix 1oz of flour into the butter used for frying, mix with water and stir well till the mixture thickens. Place into a casserole dish with ½lb of onions, ¼lb of carrots, parsley, pepper and salt. Simmer for three hours or until the ormers are tender.

When frying the ormers, onions and pork may be added, then placed with carrots, herbs and a bayleaf into a dish and slowly cooked for five to six hours.

To keep the ormers, try pickling them. After cleaning, simmer until tender, season to taste, then allow to go cold, place into a jar and cover with vinegar and seal the jar tightly.

Whichever way you choose to prepare your ormers you are guaranteed a meal with a totally different taste. Let us hope the ormer makes a return to our islands in plentiful supply so future generations can sample their unique flavour and also have the immense pleasure of low water fishing for the elusive ormer.

THE EARLY GRAMMAR SCHOOLS OF JERSEY

ONE of the secrets of prosperity in any community is education. Up to the latter part of the 15th century, Jersey had a great lack of higher education. There were primary schools in most parishes and the Church was playing its part, with many Rectors taking on the role of teachers during the weekdays.

Any gifted child would have to be sent to one of the private schools in England to continue their education. This was extremely costly, therefore only the rich families could take advantage of the opportunity, and inconvenient in the way it split up families for up to five years.

In today's world we think nothing of hopping onto a plane to travel to the mainland. In those far off days, the journey was long and arduous, and a great deal of importance was placed on the family living and working together.

The Rev. Father John Hue was instrumental in making sweeping changes in the Island's education. He was appointed Rector of St Saviour in 1461 and helped teach a few youngsters in the ancient Chapel dedicated to St Magloire, the Patron Saint of Sark. In Jersey the Saint was known as St Manelier, later changed to St Mannelier. Father John Hue also inherited a property alongside of the Chapel when his mother died. His idea was to join both properties together and form a secondary school which was good enough to end the days of youngsters travelling to England and enabling higher education to be available to a wider section of the population.

He visited Sir Richard Haliston, who was Governor of the Island of Jersey at the time, at Mont Orgueil Castle and outlined his idea. Harliston was impressed with John Hue and gave him a letter to take to the Bailiff and the Dean, part of which read: 'The schools in this Island at the moment are of poor quality, due to a lack of good masters and proper premises.'

The Bailiff, William Hamptonne, the Dean of Jersey and Bishop Herbert gave their consent to John Hue's project and he was granted two vergees and two perches of land near the Chapel on which to construct the school and a house for the Regent or headmaster. St Mannelier opened its doors to the first pupils in 1477, with the school being dedicated to St Mary Magdalen. The cost of upkeep in the early years fell heavily on the shoulders of Father Hue, who spent much of his personal fortune on the many expenses.

Help came from two Jerseymen, John Néel and Vincent Téhy, who had become successful in both business and with the Church in England. They donated towards the cost of running St Mannelier. Both men also felt another school was needed in the west of the Island, to cope with the catchment of children who found it impossible to make the daily trek to St Saviour. They chose a plot of land in St Peter alongside the Chapel of St Anastase, and obtained a Royal Charter from King Henry VII. The school of St Anastase was founded in 1496 although it didn't open its doors until October 28th, 1497, after their application had gone through the Royal Court.

Both schools flourished during the following hundred years. Subjects taught ranged from Latin, Greek, French, Arithmetic, Handwriting, Navigation, Geography, Astronomy . . . and How to Hold Text-Books. This unusual subject was included because the few books that were available were extremely expensive and beautifully bound. All teachers had to hold a licence, which in the case of grammar schools, was obtained from the Ecclesiastical Court.

Laurens Baudains tried to start a grammar school in St Helier during the early 1600s. Sir Walter Raleigh, who was Governor at that time, attempted to combine St Mannelier with this new school in town. The move failed through lack of support, and this unnamed school closed down in 1611 even though St Mannelier was in a bad state of repair and much money would be needed for it to become a responsible place of learning. Laurens Baudains remained firm in his desire to help with the education of young people in Jersey and he formed the Don Baudains Trust which still continues today to help send promising students to Oxford and Cambridge.

St Anastase, which is now a private residence.

On November 6th, 1606 the States of Jersey decided: 'That the two schools of St Mannelier and St Anastase be visited in order to test the capacity of the masters to teach, and of the children to learn, and to discover how many pupils are advanced, capable and worthy of continuing their studies for the welfare and maintainance of the Island's prosperity which is deemed very essential.'

This was to be the first report of any school inspectors ever recorded and remarkable in the fact that not only was the pupils' work to be examined, but the ability of the masters to teach would also be under scrutiny.

On September 9th, 1665 Vincent Quéron was appointed Regent of St Mannelier. His background caused some upheaval in education circles. He had been a Roman Catholic priest in France and had seduced his maid-servant. Somehow he married the girl but when she gave birth he was hauled before the Ecclesiastical Court. As no replacement could be found he was allowed to continue, but he was under immense pressure and resigned sometime between October 1666 and April 1667.

At sometime during both schools' history each was dominated by a longstanding and forceful Regent. The Pipon family held the chain of office at St Anastase for 114 years. First Pierre Pipon was headmaster from 1602 until 1664 when his son took over the running of the school until 1716.

The most famous Regent of St Mannelier was Philip Ahier. He reigned supreme from 1780 until his death on June 7th, 1832 at the age of 80. During his 52 years in charge he made many changes, including advertising in England for boarders thereby opening the doors of the school to everyone, not just Jersey children. He was a good teacher although extremely hard, and he made many enemies throughout the Island. Letters were constantly being placed in the *Gazette* demanding his removal from the school. He was also a most prolific writer of letters and none of his adversaries' letters went unanswered. During Ahier's time in charge, John Wesley visited Jersey, staying with a friend who owned a property close to St Mannelier. An after-dinner stroll took him past the school and he mentioned the ideal setting of the house, at the head of a small valley and completely surrounded by trees.

It is not certain whether corporal punishment was part of Philip Ahier's armour against disobedience from his pupils. One of his predecessors, Philippe Mattingley, had an action brought against him in the Royal Court by Nicholas Fiott. It was alleged the headmaster had beaten his son, Edward, on January 22nd, 1760, most severely. The court found in favour of the headmaster and no mention of any further action against the Regents were ever recorded.

Both schools had building problems over the 386 years they operated. In 1703 St Mannelier was partly destroyed by fire. The school house and the Regent's dwelling were both involved in the blaze, the cause of which is unknown. The States ordered a voluntary subscription from all Islanders and enough was collected for the rebuilding of the school house.

St Anastase also had problems, with the building being completely rebuilt in 1800. The foundation stone was laid on June 2nd and the States released their masons from the construction of La Rocco Tower to help finish the work. Much work was also done during 1830 at St Mannelier by the States although by this time the writing was on the wall for both establishments.

During his last few years as Regent, Philip Ahier, because of his age, had lost much of his teaching ability. The number of students declined to only six pupils during 1830. After his death, Clement Le Hardy took over and with the £500 for rebuilding granted by the States, brought the number of students up to 40 by 1835.

The final nail in the coffin came with the opening of Victoria College, in 1852. Everyone wanted to go to this new school which offered many facilities never before found in Jersey. The last pupil left St Mannelier in 1863 and both schools were forced to close their doors for the last time.

St Anastase became a private house and still bears the same name today. St Mannelier was sold and converted into flats. The money raised from the sales was used to help pay the cost of educating boys at Victoria College. So ended 386 years of grammar school education in Jersey. Whilst not perfect, many youngsters had good reason to thank Father John Hue, John Néel and Vincent Téhy for their stirling work in the field of education during the late 15th century.

THE JERSEY COW

CATTLE breeders throughout the world are united on one point. The finest milk producing cow is the Jersey. Local farmers have been exporting their cattle since the end of the 18th century, although at first the trade was mainly with England. Later the Jersey cow became famous world wide and as the demand for the best cows and bulls increased, the price rose so high that thousands more were exported annually.

The cow is a direct descendant of the prehistoric animal known as the Aurochs, Bos Primigenus, who lived during the time our ancestors dwelt in caves such as La Cotte in St Brelade. Many cave drawings remain of this animal, showing them to be extremely fierce looking beasts, standing approximately 6ft to the shoulder, with a large set of horns. The cavemen hunted this animal although the Aurochs were sufficiently large and fierce enough to turn the tables on many occasions.

By the middle of the 18th century the Jersey cow was a mixture of French, Dutch, Ayrshire, Charolais, Friesian and Brown Swiss, as cattle could be imported into the Island from anywhere. In 1763 the States of Jersey passed an Act forbidding the importation of sheep and pigs into the Island, although cattle were still being allowed in.

The cattle coming from France only stayed in the Island for a few weeks before being exported to England. This was the method French farmers used to get round the law which had placed a stiff import duty on any cows shipped to England direct from France. No such law existed between France and Jersey or Jersey and England, so the French farmers used Jersey as a stepping stone to the mainland. This method of evading import duty finally came to an end on August 8th, 1789 when the States passed the following Act: 'Whereas the fraudulent importation of cattle from France has become a most alarming matter, anyone introducing any cow, heifer, calf or bull from France should be fined 200 livres (approximately £12.50) for each animal landed, with forfeiture of boat and tackle, and the beasts should be immediately slaughtered and distributed to the poor.'

With no further importation of cattle into the Island the Jersey cow as we know it today began to take shape. A further Act passed in 1827 strengthened the previous Acts and also mentioned for the first time the term Breed of Island Cattle.

In August 1833, the Lieutenant-Governor, General Thorton, together with a group of farmers and breeders, formed the Jersey Agricultural and Horticultural Society. In December of the same year the Society received the Royal Patronage of King William IV.

The first cattle show was held in 1836 when the colour of the Jersey cow varied from white to brown or black. The black cows were known as Mulberry cows. Under the guidance of the Royal Society, selected breeding was instigated and during 1860, 1,138 cows were exported to England at an average price of £16 per head. By 1880 the price had risen to £400 per head and some exceptional cows travelled to America for £1,000 each.

In March 1866, the Royal Society started the Herd Book with the first cattle being inspected for inclusion in the book on April 4th. The first entry in the Herd Book was a grey and white bull called Dandy, who was owned by St Martin's farmer James Godfrey. Mr P. Paisnel of St Clement was the owner of the first cow included in the book. She was a light brown and white milker called Daisy.

During 1910, over a thousand head of cattle were exported to America alone. The Jersey cow was popular not only for its high milk and butter yield but because it reaches puberty at nine months and can be bred at two years. The Jersey can also survive in almost any climate, being able to withstand extreme heat and cold.

During the first half of the 20th century the Island breed grew from strength to strength with more cattle being exported than ever before. Then came the Second World War and the German occupation of the Channel Islands. In the years of occupation only half the normal number of calves were reared due to more land being used for growing wheat, potatoes and other essential crops. The Germans didn't find the taste of local meat to their liking therefore cows were imported from France and taken directly to the slaughterhouse. During the last six months of the Occupation, approximately 40 head of cattle were being sent to the abbatoir each week.

With the conclusion of the war, the Jersey cow was once again exported in large numbers to all parts of the globe. In 1949 the World Jersey Cattle Bureau was founded and they met annually in the main cattle producing countries. On the 30th anniversary in May 1979, the venue for the meeting was Jersey, with breeders from all over the world travelling to the small Island whose breed of cow had become so famous. Many of the countries present at the meeting also have their own Jersey Societies. These include South Africa, New Zealand, Australia, America, Canada and Denmark.

With careful breeding the Jersey cow has become totally free from many of the diseases that affect cattle. These include Tuberculosis, Contagious Abortion, Vibrio Foetus, Trichomoniasis, Husk (Parasitic Bronchitis), Actinobacillosis, Aclinomycosis and Leucosis.

A new idea was started in 1960 of dehorning the cattle, allowing cows to be untethered in fields and yards without damaging each other. One of the first farmers to have his herd dehorned was Mr John Bower, of Les Buttes in St Mary.

A private company set up in 1968 started the Artificial Insemination Centre and exported semen from selected bulls. The centre was later taken over by the States Committee of Agriculture and Fisheries.

With the decline in the profit of small farms, many local farmers have sold their granite farmhouses to wealthy immigrants and also sold their herds. Today there are about 146 farms on the Island, and approximately 4,200 cows are registered as milkers. Even allowing for this decline in local farming, the Jersey cow, with its high milk and butter yield is still in great demand throughout the world.

A COW'S CHRISTMAS PRAYER

MANY old Jersey farmers firmly believe their cows pray. On the stroke of midnight each Christmas Eve, superstition has it that the cattle go down on their knees in the stables to give thanks for the birth of Jesus Christ. Any human witnessing this act will, according to tradition, die before the year is out.

Numerous members of the old fraternity of local farmers still maintain the practice of bedding their cattle down before dinner on Christmas Eve, then refusing to enter the cow shed again until the following morning for fear of interrupting their animals' Christmas prayer.

THE VEGA

ON Saturday, December 30th, 1944, at 5.45 p.m. the *Vega* docked at the Albert Pier. Because darkness was descending and no announcement of her arrival had been made, there was hardly anyone present to greet the Island's most welcome visitor in 55 months. However, by the early hours of the following morning the news had spread to the whole population. To the starving Islanders it was like manna from heaven. Food parcels for all from the Red Cross ship *Vega*.

1944 had been the turning point of the War. The Allies had moved back into France, and in doing so severed the flow of food and other essential goods to the Channel Islands. Not only did the local people feel the pinch, the Germans also found themselves running short of many essential commodities. They made more demands on the farmers, and many shops found their already dwindling stocks disappearing fast. The Black Market was doing extremely well, with a few unscrupulous people growing richer by the week. Something had to be done before many people died of starvation. The Bailiffs of both Bailiwicks made an appeal in November 1944 to the General Secretary of the International Red Cross in Geneva. With the co-operation of the German and British Governments, it was agreed that a ship would sail from Lisbon with Red Cross parcels for the Channel Islands.

The Red Cross chose the 30-year-old *Vega*, a Swedish ship of 1,073 gross tonnage for the job, due to the fact that she had visited the Islands frequently before the outbreak of war carrying straw and hay for farmers. Therefore the crew would be familiar with Island waters which at times can prove dangerous. The *Vega* was due to sail from Lisbon on December 7th, thereby delivering her precious cargo in time for Christmas. Due to delays she didn't leave port until the 20th, and the population of the Islands had to search the remotest corners of their larders to find something for the Christmas table. The ship finally arrived in Guernsey on the 27th December and commenced to unload her welcome cargo.

Sunday 31st found hundreds of people trying to get near the harbour in Jersey for a better view of the *Vega*. The Germans sealed off the Albert Pier and unloading began at 8.30 a.m., with 36 volunteers, each in charge of a horse and cart, transporting the food parcels to Martlands Store in Patriotic Street. German soldiers unloaded the ship and the whole operation was supervised by the Jersey branch of St John's Ambulance Brigade. All work was suspended on New Year's Day and the task was completed on the Tuesday. Guards were posted overnight at the store, although no-one tried to break in. The parcels were then distributed to various shops for collection by the locals who had to produce the cover of their 1944 ration book to be eligible. Parcels were first handed out on January 4th, and although the Germans were starving as much as the locals, they didn't confiscate one single parcel. Some soldiers did offer to buy the contents for anything up to £30, which in those days was a great deal of money. This can be judged by a twelve-roomed house being sold for £900, and one house in Queen's Road reputedly changed hands for a chest of tea. For stealing a Red Cross parcel, one youth was sentenced to eighteen strokes of the birch, whilst another man ate so much food he had to be admitted to hospital.

The parcels had been made up by the Canadian and New Zealand Red Cross, and although there were some slight variations, the majority of the 11 lb parcels consisted of the following items: one can each of sardines, salmon, luncheon meat, corned beef, 1 lb dried milk, 1 lb butter, 1 lb jam, 5 oz chocolate, ½ lb sugar, ¼ lb cheese, 1 oz raisins, 6 oz prunes, ¼ lb tea and a small packet of mixed salt and pepper. There was also a large quantity of cigarettes, tobacco and medical supplies.

The two-man commission sent over by the Red Cross with the *Vega* was pleasantly surprised at the conditions of the Islands' inhabitants after hearing of the conditions suffered by some conquered people on the Continent. It was agreed that the *Vega* would pay regular visits which would ensure no one died of starvation. One month later, on February 6th, the ship once again docked in Guernsey and arrived in Jersey seven days later. Her third visit on March 10th saw the unloading of 5,029 sacks of flour which local bakers soon turned into loaves of bread for the patient queues of people who lined the streets outside their shops. Again on April 4th the *Vega* made her welcome visit, loaded with the life-saving food parcels.

Liberation may have brought an end to domination by the Germans, but it didn't instantly relieve the food problem. During the celebrations of early May 1945, the *Vega* quietly slipped into St Helier harbour for her fifth visit. The ship made one final call on June 8th before leaving the Channel Islands for good. During her visits the *Vega* brought a total of 478,464 food parcels and 721 tons of flour. It is difficult to imagine what the inhabitants would have done without these visits from the Red Cross. One local worker, Joseph Marie Le Guyader, who spent some time laying paving stones in the Royal Square during the Occupation, made his permanent memorial to the *Vega* by placing the stones in such a way as to spell the ship's name. The *Vega* was finally broken up in 1954 and, ironically, scrapped in Germany.

To the many people who lived through the Occupation and suffered due to the lack of food, the vision of the large white ship with a red cross on her side will remain with them forever. The Islands have good reason to support the Red Cross organisation and to fondly remember the name *Vega*.

THE SUBMERGED FOREST AND MANOR OF ST OUEN

IN every old Jersey legend there is said to be an element of truth. One story, handed down through many generations and also told by coachdrivers to eager visitors, is the tale of the sunken forest and lost manor in St Ouen's Bay.

The story of how the great forest was lost to the sea has many versions. Amongst the most colourful is the story of the "Fatal Tide." In March 709 AD a gigantic storm, which happened on an exceptionally high tide, covered all the land between England and France, leaving only elevated pinnacles of rock which became the Channel Islands.

Traces of sunken forests have been found around all the Islands. One such place is La Rocque. There is an amusing story of St Laut, Bishop of Coutances, who died in 565 AD. He told of how Jersey and France were divided by a narrow stream nine miles off La Rocque. When he visited Jersey, the locals would place a plank of wood over the stream allowing him to cross without getting his feet wet.

Another great storm, this time in 1356, is rumoured to have swallowed up both the forest and manor in St Ouen's Bay.

In the early 1500s many ships foundered on the rocks around La Corbiere. Tradition has it that the local fishermen were in cahoots with the

Seigneur and lured ships onto the rocks, thereby allowing the Seigneur to claim "Wreckage Rights." The lost area of land under the bay and the blowing of fine sand over the surrounding fertile fields was put down to divine retribution for these acts.

In 1669 the Seigneurs of Vinchelez and Morville were in conflict over wreckage rights. A certain ship had been wrecked and the exact dividing line between the two Fiefs was in question. One witness, Philippe Mahaut, aged 80, told how in his youth, during an extremely low tide, he had been shown the ruins of the Manoir de la Brecquette, which had been the property of Jean Wallis, who died in 1350, and the stumps of a vast forest, a section of which formed a straight line showing the exact boundary between the Fiefs.

The Rev. Noury, on April 6th, 1891, wrote a paper on the submerged forest and manor, placing them well out to sea in St Ouen's Bay.

On November 20th, 1908, Joseph Sinel put foward his theory on the subject. He began by discovering the depths of water surrounding each Island and then studied the animal life, finding out which species had reached certain Islands and not others. Geikie's work on the Great Ice Age also came into his reckoning. A map supposed to have been made at the end of the Ice Age showed Britain and France joined together without an English Channel. There was a large river which flowed into the Atlantic Ocean with tributaries flowing north and south. At the mouth of the river is the spot where Guernsey now lies. Sinel therefore decided it had been a gradual erosion of land by the sea, rather than a storm and sudden tidal wave, which had formed the Islands and covered all other surrounding land.

According to his calculations the speed of this process was 18 inches each century. This meant Guernsey was the first Channel Island, coming into existence some 14,000 years ago. Alderney and Sark separated from Guernsey 11,000 years ago, whilst Jersey, Herm and Jethou only came into being 4,500 years ago.

As far as the Manoir de la Brecquette and the forest is concerned, Sinel puts their disappearance from view some six centuries ago. He made extensive studies of the area and found many tree stumps, mainly of oak, alder and hazel. The size of the stumps showed the oak trees were extremely large and therefore old. He also found blocks of granite, some in disorder, whilst others had been used to make a small fishermen's jetty. He believed the Manoir had been 350 yards from the present shoreline and 120 yards south of L'Etacq Tower.

Whichever version is correct we will probably never know. One thing is certain. There was a large forest in St Ouen's Bay and Jean Wallis did live in the Manoir de la Brecquette which was situated somewhere near the forest. Exactly when and why they were swallowed up by the sea we'll have to leave to the imagination of the coachdrivers. Their stories are often better and certainly more amusing than many history books.

A KING IS PROCLAIMED

KING CHARLES I was beheaded at Whitehall on January 30th, 1649, and Oliver Cromwell, with his army of Roundheads, abolished the monarchy, leaving the Parliamentary Party in total control of England.

Before his death, Charles had managed a last meeting with his son, the Duke of York, imploring him to make good his escape before he and his elder brother could fall into the hands of the Roundheads. Dressed in female clothing the Prince of Wales, aided by Colonel Banfield, boarded a ship waiting on the Thames which transported him to Holland.

There were many people who remained loyal to the Crown, with continual battles between the Roundheads and Royalists taking place throughout

King Charles II

Britain. One of the main strongholds of the Royalists proved to be Jersey where virtually the whole Island's population remained loyal to the monarchy.

News of the King's death arrived in Jersey on February 7th and Sir George de Carteret, who literally ruled the Island as a dictator and had previously attempted to rescue Charles I from the Isle of Wight, refused to believe the story until it was confirmed by letter on the 16th. He immediately summoned the Vicomte to proclaim the Prince of Wales as King Charles II. Many of the leading Island dignitaries signed the proclamation which was read in the Market Place, now the Royal Square, on February 17th, 1649. At the conclusion of the proclamation, Sir George de Carteret raised his hat and shouted: "Long live the King." The event was preceded by the playing of drums and trumpets and was followed by a gun salute from Elizabeth Castle.

Charles was still in Holland although fears for his safety found him once again on the move. He joined his mother in Paris only to find the French unhappy with his presence in their capital. It was decided he should leave France for the only stronghold left open to him, and set sail for Jersey. He had previously visited the Island in 1646 from April 17th until June 25th, accompanied by 300 followers, so he was no stranger to our shores.

On September 17th, 1649 at 4 p.m., Charles arrived in Jersey, making his home at Elizabeth Castle in a suite of rooms which had been prepared for him. He brought his brother James, Duke of York, later to become King James II, and a large number of followers including court officials, all of whom required board and lodgings. All the church bells throughout the Island were rung until midnight, and bonfires were lit on every hilltop. The assembled craft in St Aubin's Bay fired their guns, and the cannon at the Castle once again gave a Royal Salute.

Whilst in the Island Charles is supposed to have cured many people of tuberculosis, or as it is sometimes called "King's Evil," by the laying on of hands. His easy going manner made him popular amongst the locals, and he regularly attended the Town Church for Sunday service.

On October 31st he inspected the Jersey Militia. Three thousand men at arms lined up on the sands of St Aubin's Bay, whilst Charles slowly walked between each rank. He also attended a Divine Service held at Elizabeth Castle on November 5th to praise God for the discovery of the Gunpowder Plot. He left the Island on February 13th, 1650.

On May 8th, 1660, eleven years after he had been proclaimed King Charles II in the Market Place of St Helier, he was anointed King of England in London. On June 2nd the news reached Jersey and Edouard Hamptonne went to the Market Place and for the second time proclaimed Charles King in Jersey.

Here follows a translation of the proclamation and a list of the people who signed:

Sir George de Carteret

So it was that the rebels, through a dreadful coup, have put their violent hands on Charles I of glorious memory, through the death of whom the sovereign crowns of England, Scotland, France and Ireland belong, and will be inherited solely and legally by His Royal Highness and powerful Prince Charles. To these effects the Lieutenant-Governor and Bailiff and Jurats of the Island of Jersey, assisted by the officers of the King of this Island, all in accord publish and proclaim that His Highness the very powerful Prince Charles has now, after the death of the Sovereign of glorious memory, become through the legal right of succession and hereditary line, our only and legal Sovereign, Charles II, by the Grace of God, King of England, Scotland, France and Ireland; defender of the faith, to whom we recognise having to obey, honour and be faithful to; and we pray God, by the Grace of whom Kings reign, to affirm Charles II with all his rights and on this throne and to make him reign a long time and happily upon us; and so be it.

Long live King Charles II

1649, the 17th of February.

George de Carteret; Phil de Carteret; Amice de Carteret; Francois de Carteret; Josue de Carteret; Elie Dumaresq; Ph. Le Geyt; Jean Pipon; Pierre Fautrart; Josue Palot; Helier de Carteret; Laurens Hamptonne; Jean Le Hardy; Philipe Dumaresq; Edouard Romeril; Jean Seale; Jacques Guillaume; Nicholas Richardson; Nicholas Journeaux; Isaac Herault; Jean Le Couteur; Abraham Bigg; Helier Hue.

FORT d'AUVERGNE

DURING the early part of the 18th century, a guard house was built between Havre des Pas and La Collette against possible attacks by the French. It was first mentioned in reports during the Seven Years War (1756-1763) when an order for a further supply of ammunition was made. The battery was manned by eight soldiers supervised by one sergeant.

In 1788 the States ordered the Constable of St Helier, Edouard Patriarche, to hire the necessary labour to construct a powder magazine and a platform on which two cannon could be mounted. He was given the sum of £25 to pay for the construction although, on completion, he had to ask the States for a further eight pounds and two shillings in order to settle the accounts.

The small fortification eventually ceased to be of any significance and it was demolished just after the beginning of the 20th century. The existence of the building would probably have been lost in the passing of time had it not been for Major-General James d'Auvergne.

Jersey has a history of naming various places after people who have made a great contribution to the Island. The small battery at Havre des Pas was given the name of Fort d'Auvergne in recognition of the many services to Jersey by the Major-General.

James d'Auvergne was born in St Helier in 1726 and was one of three children whose father, Charles, died in 1729 when James was only three. The family were direct descendants of the Count of Auvergne whose family motto was "Nous ne changeons pas — we do not change".

Although James moved to England, living in Southampton, he never forgot his native Island, and after a distinguished military career he represented the States of Jersey as Deputy in England from 1756-1759. On numerous occasions he pleaded with the Privy Council on behalf of the Island, and one of his successes was obtaining twelve cannon in 1758. At his own expense, repair work was carried out on the statue of King George II in the Royal Square, which had been built in 1751 by the sculptor John Cheere. Further work was also done to the railings which enclosed the statue, a gift from the Lieutenant-Governor, Colonel William Deane, to preserve the monument from 18th century graffiti.

In 1759 he purchased the two chapels built on the mound at La Hougue Bie and had a tall brick tower constructed on the roof of the chapels from which he could look out over the Island. In 1792, James gave this now famous plot of land — the prehistoric tomb under the mound had not then been discovered — to his nephew Philippe d'Auvergne, who became famous as the Duke of Bouillon.

James d'Auvergne and his wife, Elisabeth Mauger, stayed in Southampton until his death in 1799 at the age of 73. During his last years he had been Sheriff of Southampton in 1792 and Mayor of the city in 1795.

In 1923 the Cabeldu family bought the house which had been constructed on the site of the old fort and converted it into an hotel. In order to continue the tradition of honouring the famous sons of Jersey, they called their hotel Fort d'Auvergne, therefore ensuring that the small battery which once guarded the shoreline and the name of James d'Auvergne would be remembered by many generations to come.

GALLOWS HILL

THE devastating storm of October 1987 which decimated the tree population of Westmount, as well as many other places, brought back into public view the small building consisting of four pillars and a roof which once housed the King's Gallows where many wrong-doers met their fate at the end of a rope.

Public hangings began at Gallows Hill, known as Mont es Pendus or Le Mont Patibulaire (the mount of hanging), at the beginning of the 17th century. Many unfortunate people were marched there from the prison at Charing Cross to Westmount, accompanied by large crowds of onlookers. Whenever there was to be an execution the locals would treat it as a public holiday, with even the schoolchildren attending the event.

The most remarkable of these occasions took place on Saturday, April 25th, 1807, when William Hales was taken to Gallows Hill for execution. He was a Private in the 34th Regiment of the Light Infantry which was stationed in the Island. Hales had been found guilty of breaking into the watchmaking

Prospect of the Towne of St. Hillary Bay and Castles taken from the land

shop of Mr Pierre Poignard of St Helier, and of committing a burglary. The Royal Court took the unusual step of passing the death sentence for what was a common, everyday crime. A vast crowd had gathered, including many of his fellow soldiers and officers of the Regiment, to watch the hangman, Jean Vasseline from France, perform his duty. The bolt was pulled and the trap door opened. Hales was left hanging for a few minutes when Jean Vasselin noticed he was still breathing. In order to save the man any further suffering, Vasselin grabbed hold of Hales around the legs and added his weight to the rope.

This only resulted in the rope being stretched and Hales was able to touch the ground with his feet. Vasselin then climbed on the shoulders of the convicted man in an effort to finish the execution. This stretched the rope even more, allowing Hales to stand firmly on the ground.

William Hales then opened his eyes and gazed at the astounded gathering. Somehow his hands had come untied and he removed the noose from around his neck. There were mixed feelings amongst the crowd as to whether a second attempt should be made or whether the man should be set free. Hales was taken back to prison whilst his case was reviewed. Eventually a free pardon was granted by King William, and Hales returned to England where he married, raised a family, kept himself well within the law and lived to see old age. He became known as "The Man Jersey Couldn't Hang."

The hangman was more successful in the case of Philippe Jolin. After returning from a drinking spree he had an argument with his father, which ended with him throwing a brick which hit the older man on the back of the head and killed him. This event, on September 7th, 1829, resulted in Philippe facing a charge of murder. He was found guilty and sentenced to be hanged on Saturday, October 3rd. Over 200 people followed him on his last walk from the prison to Gallows Hill where a further 6,000 had gathered. Philippe had shown great remorse over the death of his father, blaming alcohol for his downfall. Whilst he stood on the scaffold he faced the crowd and, in a firm voice, addressed them as follows:

"You see where drink has led me. I hope that you will benefit from my experience by not giving way to drink, by so doing we crucify Jesus Christ, and yes we crucify the Saviour of the World. I admit that I deserve this sentence of mine but I hope that God's Grace will always be with me."

He then took hold of the New Testament and read aloud the 1st Chapter of the First Epistle of St Peter, starting at Verse 3. In front of a strangely hushed crowd, Philippe Jolin was hanged by the neck until dead.

The hangman was paid 25 crowns a year for his service and lived in a rent-free cottage. After every hanging he also collected 3d from every stallholder in the market, and his other perk of the job was being allowed to keep the clothes of the victims. The office of public hangman was abolished on December 11th following a petition to the States by the Constable of St Helier.

Gallows Hill ceased to be used for public hangings with subsequent death sentences carried out at Newgate Street prison. On Saturday, August 11th, 1866, a 20-year-old Jerseyman, Francis Bradley, was sent to meet his maker. Over 15,000 people turned up to watch the spectacle, some waiting all night outside the prison doors in order to obtain a good view. On the houses facing the prison wall, platforms had been erected for the friends and families of the owners to have a grandstand view. Bradley's body remained on the gallows for the statutory one hour before being laid to rest in the grounds of the prison and covered with quicklime.

Gallows Hill as it is today, enjoying pleasant views over the Bay, while on the previous page the not-so-pleasant view afforded to its victims in the 17th century.

The last public hanging was of Joseph Philippe Le Brun, aged 52, from St Lawrence. He was charged with shooting his sister Nancy and wounding his brother-in-law, Philippe Laurens, on December 15th, 1874. Right until the last he professed his innocence, and there were many who believed him. Nevertheless on Thursday, August 12th at 8 a.m. he kept his appointment with the hangman. After the statutory hour on the gallows, a woman approached a warder asking if she could touch the corpse. She believed him to be innocent, and felt if she touched the body with her withered arm, then she would be healed. Her request was denied.

The last person to hang in Jersey was Frank Huchet on Friday, October 9th, 1959. This 32-year-old Jerseyman had been found guilty of shooting John Perrée in the face, then burying his body in the sand dunes at Mont à la Brune, St Brelade. Around 100 people were present outside the prison gates as the final execution took place. Since then the rope has been kept in the locker and Gallows Hill has become a place for courting couples instead of a place of death.

THE CHANNEL ISLANDS' FIRST AIRPORT

JERSEY AIRPORT was very much in the public eye when it celebrated its 50th anniversary. Royal visitors, Concorde, the Red Arrows, plus hundreds of private aircraft paraded before the interested crowds. But when the first airport in the Channel Islands became 50-years-old, in 1986, the event seemed to pass almost unnoticed in Jersey and Guernsey. The people of Alderney, however, celebrated the opening of Blaye Airport with the knowledge that others may do things on a larger scale, but the tiny, most northern isle has the distinction of being the first to have an operational airport in the Channel Islands.

Among the people who gathered at the airport for the celebrations was one person who had more memories of the early days of flying than any of the others present. Mrs Wilma Bragg was the first Airport Controller, ticket seller, baggage handler, aircraft loader and girl Friday. In fact she virtually ran Blaye Airport single-handed. At just 22 years of age she had been chosen by Jersey Airlines to become the first woman in charge of an airport in Britain.

On April 1st, 1935, Judge Meelish, accompanied by Jurats of the Alderney Court, turned the first sod before allowing the tractors to take over the task of levelling out the airstrip. It had been hoped to commence operations some time during August of that year, but delays occurred and the date was gradually postponed until Friday, March 27th, 1936, when Jersey Airlines flew to Alderney with just two paying passengers. The first to purchase his ticket and land was Mr Gordon Rice from Jersey. Although this was the first commercial landing in Alderney, it wasn't the first actual landing. In September 1935 an inspector had arrived from Guernsey to check the runway.

Alderney Airport was the brainchild of Harold G. Benest, a Jerseyman who ran Bellingham Travel and Jersey Airlines. Together with Jurat Le Cocq of Alderney, they negotiated with 40 Alderney residents who owned small parcels of land around Blaye for the lease of what was mostly barren headland. Harold Benest also built the Grand Hotel in Alderney, thereby introducing tourism to the Island.

Wilma Le Cocq — she was not married until during the War — was the daughter of Jurat Le Cocq, and was offered the job of running the small airport. She received six weeks training in Jersey where the aircraft were still

De Havilland Dragons lined up on Jersey's West Park beach.

using West Park beach. She then set up home in the tiny shed provided as an airport building. Inside the shed her working area was a wooden bench balanced on top of two 50-gallon oil drums. There was no official opening ceremony, Wilma just got down to work without any cutting of ribbons or speeches. Aircraft arrived at 8.15 a.m. and 6.30 p.m. every Sunday, Monday, Wednesday and Friday, with a scheduled turnaround time of ten minutes. In between flights Wilma was kept busy running the small office in St Anne from where she sold tickets, typed letters and kept the books.

To help with some of the heavy work, Wilma enlisted the aid of a pensioner, Sam Allen. He would mow the grass and help carry the baggage to the aircraft in a wheelbarrow. Sam was also helped by the local taxi-driver, Sid Simon, to man the fire brigade at the airport. This consisted of an open car with three fire extinguishers on the back seat. The customs officer was a retired Lieutenant Commander who didn't check the baggage but scrutinised the passports of anyone who wasn't British. This was the entire staff of what was, and probably still is, one of the smallest commercial airports in Britain.

Wilma still lives in Alderney and recalls the early days of aviation. There were no phones on Alderney at the time, so all messages had to be sent by telegram. This would usually work satisfactorily, although some unscheduled aircraft sometimes landed at Blaye. The pilots would fly around the Island to attract Wilma's attention, and she would leave whatever she was doing and rush to the airport in the company car so they could land. On one particular Bank Holiday there was a carnival in St Anne, and Wilma was taking part on a float depicting Henry VIII and his wives. Wilma was dressed as Anne Boleyn when an aircraft circled the Island. She rushed to the airport and pushed the steps out to the aircraft. Alderney is sometimes accused of being behind the times, but an aircraft met by Anne Boleyn did startle the few passengers.

Weather reports also caused some problems. If the grass airstrip was hit by a sudden downpour of rain, Wilma and Sam would put on their wellington boots and go out to inspect the runway. On occasions it would be too late to send a telegram to stop the incoming aircraft, so Wilma would stand in the middle of the runway and wave a white towel at the pilot, who would then turn back.

Another part of her job would be to remove the grazing cows from the runway when an aircraft was due. Any passengers who arrived and needed the urgent use of a toilet had to be directed to the nearest gorse bushes because the airport didn't have the necessary facilities. Wilma would also go round every Christmas to pay rent to the 40 landowners on whose land the airport was built. Her employment as Airport Controller was indeed more interesting and varied than her previous job, which had been school teacher to 18 six-year-olds at the old school, which now houses the local museum.

All good things have to come to an end, and the German Occupation saw the end of Wilma's employment at Blaye Airport. Along with all other Islanders she was evacuated to England where she handed in the books at the London office of Jersey Airlines. The pilots and staff were all joining the Fleet Air Arm, and Wilma was persuaded to join them. She became a Wren and served along with many other Channel Islanders during the Second World War. She didn't return to Alderney until 1948, by which time her sister had taken over the responsibility of running Blaye Airport.

Aurigny have long since taken over Blaye Airport, and the Rapides have given way to Trislanders. The buildings have been modernised with hangars and toilets, and fire engines have replaced the old fire extinguishers. Even so, there is still a certain magic about landing at Alderney Airport, and I'm sure Wilma Bragg still looks to the sky every time she hears an aircraft circling the Island.

GEOFFROY'S LEAP

A FAMOUS landmark between Gorey Castle and Anne Port Bay is that of Geoffroy's, or Jeoffroy's, Leap. No one knows who the mysterious Geoffroy was or even if he ever really existed. Two different versions of how he came to leap off the rock are told.

Firstly he was supposed to have been a prisoner in the castle and somehow managed to escape. He was chased along the cliffs, and before the

Geoffroy's Leap — a wonderful legend.

soldiers could catch him he leapt off the rock and swam ashore. Everyone was so amazed that he had survived the jump from such a height that he was offered his freedom if he repeated the feat. Geoffroy agreed, although by this time the tide had started to recede and his second leap took him onto the rocks and to his death.

The more popular story tells how Geoffroy was found guilty of a crime against a woman. He had a reputation in the parish for his flirtations with the opposite sex and this time had overstepped the mark. He was sentenced to be thrown off the cliffs to his death on the rocks below. At the appointed hour he was escorted to the place of execution by two halberdiers, and a masked executioner pushed him off the cliff.

A large crowd had gathered to witness the event, mostly women who wanted to see an end to the man who chased their daughters, but also many daughters who were weeping at losing this good-looking man to the keeping of the waters.

To their astonishment he missed the rocks and came ashore at Anne Port. There were some who cried out for his release as his survival must have proved his innocence, whilst others wanted him pushed off again so that justice could be done. Geoffroy saw a method of gaining favour with many of the young ladies present, and in a rash moment declared he would leap off the rock of his own free will. The second attempt met with disaster as he hit the rocks, breaking not only his head, but many hearts as well.

We will never know the whole truth of Geoffroy's Leap, but the second and best known version is a wonderful legend of how far a man will go to please the ladies.

THE BLACK DOG OF BOULEY BAY

THE large Black Dog of Bouley Bay is just one of numerous legends of Jersey. Usually these legends were either made up by superstitious people and enlarged upon over the years, or began as insignificant incidents which were blown up out of all proportion. In the case of the Black Dog of Bouley Bay, there is an extremely sound reason for the telling of the story during the latter half of the 18th century. The reason was smuggling.

Stories were circulated that a large black dog with huge saucer shaped eyes roamed around Bouley Bay pulling its chain behind it. If anyone heard the sound of the chain they would be so petrified that they would be unable to run away from the approaching dog. Once the animal had caught his victim he would circle round the unfortunate person at great speed with the chain making a dreadful noise. Although no actual bodily harm was ever done to anyone, the victims of these attacks were found cowering against a hedge in such a state that a large amount of brandy was required to repair the damage done by meeting the Black Dog.

Therefore the slightest mention that the dog had been heard was enough to send everyone hurrying to their homes, leaving a clear path for the smugglers to move their contraband from the harbour to its intended destination.

Smuggling was common practice amongst the fishermen of the time. They could arrange a meeting, probably on the Ecréhous, with a fellow fisherman from France, and an exchange of goods could be made well away from any prying eyes.

One such fisherman was Frainque Desclios who was drowned when he fell into the harbour. His small cottage at the foot of Bouley Bay was considered too small for him to lie in state. Therefore it was decided to move his coffin to

Bouley Bay with what is now the Waters Edge Hotel at the foot.

the office of the undertaker of the parish. This particular gentleman was also the smugglers' main distributor of goods. A number of Frainque's fellow fishermen accordingly arrived at his cottage with a horse and cart and loaded the coffin, covering it with a large black cloth. The undertaker had in fact provided two coffins, and the horse had a heavy load to pull up the hill that day. Frainque Desclios lay in state and was visited by his many grieving friends and relations. The church service was well attended and after the burial a great deal of brandy was consumed to wish him a safe and speedy journey to the promised eternal life in heaven.

A few hours later the undertaker discovered that the wrong coffin had been taken to the church and thereafter buried in the graveyard. That evening a rumour was circulated concerning the Black Dog, and how he had been heard roaming around the vicinity of the church. Everyone took to their homes, and the men with spades were not disturbed whilst they gave Frainque a somewhat belated funeral and retrieved their precious coffin of contraband. Once again the Black Dog of Bouley Bay had done its work in frightening off any passers-by.

LE VESCONTE MONUMENT

ON December 21st, 1837, the Le Vesconte family of Trinity received an early Christmas present—the gift of a son whom they decided to name Philippe. He was the only son and grew up at the family home of La Porte with his sisters. The Le Vesconte family had always taken a great interest in the affairs of Trinity, and many of the Honorary positions of the parish had, for years, been filled by members of their family. Philippe was to be no exception.

He grew to be extremely tall, and although a man of few words, Philippe proved himself to be a good administrator. He entered the Honorary Police and soon worked his way up to Centenier. In 1868, he fought his first election for Constable, and at the young age of 31 he followed in his father's footsteps and became head of the parish. He retained this position until 1877 when he relinquished the office. During his time in office he had kept the rates down to just a few pence, and had become the figurehead of the whole parish, feared by a few although revered by the majority because of his straight speaking and down to earth way of dealing with problems.

The whole family gathered at La Porte each Sunday and, with Philippe at its head, would walk down to the parish church. At this time Trinity had a Rector who enjoyed the pleasures of the bottle. On numerous occasions he had trouble in performing his duties. Getting in and out of the pulpit had become a hazardous business on Sunday evenings. Watching the antics of the drunken Rector did not amuse Philippe, and one Sunday as he marched his family down to church he decided this was the Rector's last chance. As it happened the Rector found the steps to the pulpit too much to handle, and Philippe Le Vesconte stood up and led his family out of the church and up the road to the small Methodist chapel of Ebenezer, passing through the door just as the last hymn was being sung. From that moment the Le Vesconte family became Methodists. Philippe didn't find the small chapel grand enough, so he set about rebuilding it by donating money, plus loaning workers and a horse and cart to move stone. A plaque inside the chapel tells how he was the secretary of Ebenezer from 1883 until 1891 when he became treasurer until 1909.

In 1890 a deputation called on Philippe Le Vesconte and once again he stood for Constable. He duly won the election and remained in office until his death in 1909. During his time as Constable he fought seven elections, winning the support of the vast majority of the parish each time. Before his wife collapsed and died in the yard of La Porte while collecting vegetables, she had borne him a son and three daughters. His son helped in the affairs of the parish, becoming the senior Centenier and therefore second in command to his father. During his second term as Constable, the parish presented Philippe with a set of silverware and a parchment scroll, the text of which follows:

To Mr Ph. Le Vesconte; of Trinity; Sir;

We the undersigned wish to tender a deep and spontaneous expression of our grateful thanks for the eminent and valuable service you have rendered to this parish.

It was as long ago as 1868, at a relatively early age, you were called upon to direct the affairs of the parish.

In 1871 and again in 1874 the electors renewed your mandate. After having relinquished the helm for several years you were called upon to assume the duties of the office once more, and last year your mandate was renewed for the fifth time. You have, by your wise and good administration and your great self-sacrifice, merited the respect and esteem of your parishioners. We have been given the opportunity to appreciate the very real qualities which form the basis of your character. The courtesy with which one is always received in your home, the strength of your convictions are equalled only by your great modesty.

Let us also remember in passing that you are the eldest member of the Legislative Assembly of this Bailiwick, and that there, as elsewhere you have always stood for the real interests of the Island. We have noted with pleasure that you have always opposed those who would want to abolish our privileges, our traditions and our liberties. You have always a lively interest in the many and

Unveiling of memorial to Mr Philippe Le Vesconte, Constable of Trinity 1868-1909, in July 1910.

varied affairs of the municipality. Under your intelligent direction the wheels of administration have run smoothly and even though the workload has increased it has appeared lighter to all concerned. The care of the parish finances has brought forth in you a masterly quality; Economy. We cannot allow to pass unnoticed the fact that your father had, before you, held the high office which you now hold, and that Mr Philippe Le Vesconte, your son, has for the last eight years been the senior Centenier of this parish.

It is our sincere wish that the Almighty will bless you and the members of your family with a long and happy life.

We take the opportunity on this occasion to ask you respectfully to accept these articles of silverware as a testimony of our thanks for the distinguished service you have rendered to our parish and our Island.

The committee for and in the name of the 282 subscribers; John Norman; John Le Gros; Philippe Cabot; Francois Dorey; Josue Picot; Richard Blampied; Ph. Aubin Jnr; Denis Blampied; Philippe Gallichan; Chs Sydney Le Gros; E.G. Le Quesne; Charles de Gruchy; Chs Wm Blampied Jnr; Jean Benest; Philippe de Gruchy; Philippe Deslandes; Peter Le Feuvre; John Godeaux; F.S. Gibaut; Clement Pinel; Thomas Cabot;

The 18th day of October 1894.

During the early half of 1909 Philippe Le Vesconte contracted pleurisy, and concern about his health was felt throughout the parish. He made a slight recovery during the summer months, then had a relapse. At 1 o'clock on the morning of August 21st, Philippe Le Vesconte finally ceased to be father of the parish he had served for over 40 years. He died in his 72nd year at his home, La Porte, and was laid out on the bed enabling the many relatives to go and place a kiss on the forehead of the man who had ruled the family. A great era in the history of the parish of Trinity had ended.

Over 300 people attended his funeral, including 100 schoolchildren, who marched from Trinity School to La Porte. They lined up on either side of the entrance as the coffin was carried out. The children then hurried to the chapel where they once again formed two lines as guard of honour for the entry of the body into the chapel. The service was conducted by the Rev. H. Foss, after which the entire congregation walked behind the hearse to Cimetière de L'Union at St. Martin's Arsenal. As the coffin was placed into the family vault, the schoolchildren sang a hymn, bringing tears to the eyes of everyone present.

On June 28th, 1910, a large gathering took place at the crossroads near La Porte where a monument had been constructed in honour of the man who had devoted his life to both his parish and his Island. The unveiling ceremony was attended by the Bailiff, Sir William Vernon, and many other parish and Island dignitaries. After the unveiling the party walked to the Bouley Bay Hotel, which has since been demolished, to celebrate the memory of Philippe Le Vesconte, father of Trinity.

HOWARD DAVIS PARK

THOMAS BENJAMIN FREDERICK DAVIS was born on April 25th, 1867, at Havre des Pas, and as his father was a local fisherman, he grew up with the sea in his blood. Therefore it came as no surprise when, at the age of 14, he left Jersey and went to sea. He learnt all the arts of sailing until settling down in South Africa where he made his fortune, owning all the major stevedoring services between Durban and Mombasa.

As with most Islanders, he never forgot his homeland and returned to settle down in the Island he loved. He married Minne Bagge and the couple had seven children, although sadly three died in infancy. During the First World War he lost his favourite son, Howard Leopold, in whose memory he set up the Howard Leopold Davis Scholarship Trust to help local youngsters through further education, especially if they wished to enter the armed forces. He also gave the property known as 'Parkfield' to the States of Jersey in 1928 which has since been turned into an experimental farm to aid local farmers and growers.

'Plaisance'

In 1937, Sir Bertram Falle, later to become Lord Portsea, put his 10 acre property 'Plaisance' on the market for £25,000. This consisted of a large mansion surrounded by an expansive garden. T.B. Davis decided this would make an excellent park and bought the property. Most of the buildings were demolished, and under the guidance of Mr James Darling Colledge, the landscaping of the park began early in 1938.

The main entrance had an ornate arch with high railings on each side, and an army of expert gardeners set about laying the great lawn surrounded by flower beds and secluded pathways. Just inside the entrance T.B. Davis placed a bronze statue of his great friend, King George V, sculpted by Sir William Reid-Dick. T.B. Davis had become a great yachtsman and in his J-class schooner *Westward* had raced against the King many times. His vast collection of trophies can be seen in the Jersey Museum along with photographs of his racing yachts.

The official handing over of the park to the people of Jersey took place on Saturday September 30th, 1939, when in the presence of the Bailiff, later Lord Coutanche, and many other Island dignitaries, T.B. Davis made the following speech:

"Mrs Davis and I present Jersey with this park in memory of our son Howard, who gave his life for his King in the Great War at the Battle of the Marne, and I will ask all people who visit this park to respect his memory and do nothing that would not be in keeping with his wishes. I only make two requests, and I trust these will be granted by the representative of our Island on behalf of the people. Firstly, that the little hall on the left of the entrance will be kept for all time for the housing of our son's picture which is to be installed there. Secondly, that at no time will this park be built upon except for such building as may be necessary for a park or for the benefit of the people who use the park."

Within a few years the Island came under the occupation of Germany and a few changes were made at the park. At first it remained a quiet refuge until the shortage of food caused the great lawn to be ploughed up for the growing of maincrop potatoes. This took place on June 17th, 1943. Later in that year, a small cemetery appeared in the park to accommodate the bodies of British and American servicemen who were washed ashore from *HMS Charybdis* and *HMS Limbourne*. A granite plaque in the cemetery reads:

"This cemetery was dedicated on 26th November 1943, as a resting place for the bodies of members of the Allied Forces recovered within the Bailiwick during the Second World War."

The crosses in this cemetery are made of oak from a tree donated by a lady who lived at Grainville Manor, where the school now stands. The crosses were made by Messrs Le Seeleur the builders, who also undertook their cleaning and general maintenance for many years. Although the bodies of the Americans have since been removed, the cemetery is overlooked by the War Graves Commission and remains the only war cemetery with oak crosses. Recently many of the crosses had to be renewed and an oak tree from La Haule was used for the purpose.

There is also a memorial in the park to the 2,000-plus Jersey internees who were sent to concentration camps throughout Europe.

To celebrate the 50th anniversary of the purchase of the property, a floral clock was installed in a flower bed close to the statue of King George.

On September 27th, 1942, at the age of 75, T.B. Davis died in Durban. In accordance with his wishes, his yacht *Westward* was sunk in the Hurd Deep, although the original spinnaker boom now stands high in the park where it is used as a flagpole.

The only part of the original building of Plaisance has been turned into the Howard Hall where the portrait of Howard Leopold Davis by Jessie Hilson can be viewed.

Today the park is still used as a place of peace and tranquillity by locals and holidaymakers alike. Many top bands entertain free of charge throughout the summer months and the gardens have been maintained to a standard which would make T.B. Davis justly proud of his gift to the people of Jersey.

War Cemetery, Howard Davis Park.

JERSEY RACES

HORSE RACING, the sport of Kings, has been active in Jersey for well over 150 years. Sir John Le Couteur, A.D.C. for the Sovereign in Jersey, encouraged the breeding of horses for racing as they would also be useful for pulling the guns of the Militia. Up to this time all the horses in the Island had been bred for use on the farms and racing was confined to the horses of the troops for the garrison and the few wealthy English gentlemen who resided in Jersey. With Sir John's backing, many farmers bred one or two horses especially for the races and the general public responded to this new sport by flocking in their thousands to the various meetings.

Race meetings were run at various venues, usually lasting two days, and were accompanied by numerous side shows and drinking tents. The main venue was Gorey Common, where tents were erected on either side of the track for spectators to partake of both liquid refreshment and more substantial lunches. Many booths were provided for betting, and due to the close proximity of the booths to the race track, there were numerous accidents when horses bolted.

Racing on Grouville Common, July 1849, from a painting by P. J. Ouless.

Not everyone was pleased with the races. One parson preached from his pulpit to his congregation about the "enormous iniquity of horse racing" and pleaded with them not to attend such outings. Also the foreman in charge of the gang of Irish workers, who were building St Catherine's Breakwater, was not amused when his entire workforce took the day off to go to the races at Gorey Common.

The races moved to Gorey in 1843, before which they had been held at Greve d'Azette and previously on St Aubin's beach. Whilst at Greve d'Azette most spectators viewed the races, for a small entrance charge, from Mr Rose's promenade. A grandstand, which doubled as a band stand, had been erected and the racing took place on the sands. Also during race week, various wrestling and rifle competitions plus boxing matches were arranged in the many booths which surrounded the promenade. Ladies were only admitted if they had previously applied for a card of admission.

During this period the races were covered by the *Jersey Journal and Fashionable Gazette* which started on Saturday, March 18th, 1837, and folded, after 39 issues, on Saturday, December 9th of the same year. This journal is a mine of information regarding the races held at Greve d'Azette. From various pieces of reporting we learn that on Wednesday August 3rd, 1837, one horse which took part in a race was later arrested by the Sheriff. His crime was unknown! On the same day there was a fight between a mob of locals and some soldiers. A few of the soldiers drew their bayonets to defend themselves whilst a less fortunate soldier was chased by the mob over a 12ft high wall from which he fell into 4ft of water.

The Race Ball and Race Dinner always seemed to be a dismal affair with few people bothering to attend. Judging by the number of beer and fine wine booths positioned in the area around the races, it is probable that most of the spectators were too much the worse for wear to be able to attend any evening celebrations.

Even in those days a good horse could fetch a great deal of money. Mr Gaudin's horse Young Selim won the Queen's Cup during August 1837 and was later sold to an English gentleman for £50.

Mr Gillingham was another local breeder who had a great deal of success. On Tuesday, April 11th, 1837, two of his horses — Panther and Dolly Mop — were placed first and second in the opening race of the day, although the only other competitor — Mildred — was reported as being "fit for the knacker's yard." Mr Gillingham then went on to win the Hunter's Stakes with Brown Stout after his sole rival threw his rider and was unable to be caught.

One of the first major races was the King's Cup which was started in 1836. This race was open to horses bred in Jersey, and although the race continued to be run, the trophy never arrived from England. In 1841 it became known as the Queen's Plate, though whether or not the original trophy ever turned up is not reported.

Special boats from Guernsey made the races at Grouville a true inter-insular event.

After the races were moved to Gorey the event took on massive proportions, as can be judged by the painting hanging in the Museum. A special boat was chartered for people wishing to come from Guernsey and the numerous races included Her Majesty's Cup, The Drag Hunt Cup, and the main event, The Island's Club Plate. Lillie Langtry was only one of the famous visitors to Gorey Common during race week. Her first introduction to the Sport of Kings came at an early age, no doubt having a great influence on her later love of the sport and her involvement with the breeding of many of her own horses, which she raced under the assumed name of "Mr Jersey."

Racing continued at Gorey for 60 years, although during this time there were also race meetings held at Les Landes and the well attended Trinity Races at Jardin d'Olivet which were under the patronage of His Excellency Major-General H. Wray, C.M.G. R.E., Lieutenant-Governor of Jersey. The starter, Mr Nicolas Mollet, had a busy afternoon at Trinity with seven races being held between 1 p.m. and 5 p.m. These included the Galloway Race, the Trinity Cup, the Town Plate, the Farmer's Cup plus races for ponies, with the prize money ranging from 6 to 10 guineas.

On certain occasions there were private races run during race week. One such event took place in 1884 between Mr E.J. Le Blancq's Butterfly and Mr T. Cabot's Trinity Boy. Each owner put up 10 sovereigns with the winner taking the prize.

Many of the locally-bred horses faired well against those of the English gentry, due to the introduction in the 1800s of the strain of horses brought to the Island by the Russians, who stayed here until the sea around the Russian coastline unfroze and they were able to return to their homeland. This meant the Island breed became mixed with a cossack strain which added greatly to their speed.

Jersey races have come a long way since their conception. The many spectators who went to St Aubin's sands on June 1st, 1835, to watch five races, the most valuable being the Jersey Purse worth £25, would find a marked difference to the race track at Les Landes.

Seven thousand people witnessed the hurdle race at Greve d'Azette on August 5th, 1837, when officers of the 60th Royal Rifles gave a cup for a two horse race over two heats, with Maid of the West beating Irish Girl in both heats by a nose. They would find a big difference in the much larger field of horses today, which have the added bonus of many top English riders such as the Princess Royal taking part.

From St Aubin to Greve d'Azette, then Gorey Common, Jardin d'Olivet, Les Quennevais and finally Les Landes, the Jersey Races have covered most of the Island. They now seem settled at Les Landes where the going must be better than the sands, and viewing a great deal easier and more comfortable than Mr Rose's promenade, although it is doubtful if they attract as many spectators as the 7,000 who used to gather at Greve d'Azette.

QUEEN'S ASSEMBLY ROOMS

THE Queen's Assembly Rooms in Belmont Road were opened in August 1851 and were housed in what was, at that time, the largest building in St Helier.

The Jersey Times gives the opening date as Monday 4th, although this was delayed until the Tuesday because the Dustin Family, who were to provide the musical entertainment, were delayed in London.

This was the Dustin Family's second visit to Jersey. The ensemble consisted of Mr and Mrs Theodore Dustin, Mr H. Dustin, Mr W. Dustin and Mr R. A. Brown, who accompanied them on the pianoforte. The family were renowned for their playing of the sax-horns, and they used silver horns presented to them by Louis Philippe in Paris during 1844. They also performed on the newly invented euphonic horns, with Mrs Dustin leading the group with her vocal expertise. Front stalls for the performance were four shillings, with a ticket for a family of four priced at twelve shillings. Back stalls were two shillings and children were allowed in at half price.

Apart from concerts and banquets, the Queen's Assembly Rooms were also the venue for many public meetings. One such meeting was held on Saturday, October 13th, 1855, and had far reaching effects. The French

Once the largest building in St Helier, the Queen's Assembly Rooms.

weekly paper in Jersey, called *L'Homme,* had on Wednesday, October 10th, published an open letter by Félix Pyat to Queen Victoria following her visit to Napoleon III in Paris. Part of the letter read: "You have sacrificed your dignity as a Queen, your fastidiousness as a woman, your pride as an aristocrat, even your honour."

Nicholas Le Quesne, Connétable of St Helier, chaired the meeting which began at 7.15 p.m. and the crowd of between 1,500 and 2,000 expressed their horror at the deplorable letter and called for the expulsion from Jersey of the three men responsible for publishing *L'Homme,* Ribeyrolles, Pianciani and Thomas. By October 19th all three men had left the Island and a group of "Proscrits" met at Marine Terrace, home of Victor Hugo, where the great writer had prepared a declaration in support of the publishers of *L'Homme.*

A total of 27 people signed the declaration which ended with the line; "And now, expel us."

Their wish was duly granted and Victor Hugo left Jersey on October 31st at 7.15 a.m. on board the *Courier,* and landed in Guernsey at 10 a.m.

The Assembly Rooms consisted of a ballroom with a flight of wide stone stairs leading to a long gallery room upstairs with a platform at one end. The room was lit by branched candlesticks and gas chandeliers, which still remain today. Kine's Brewery took over the Room and, during 1876, ran it as a skating saloon which opened daily with evening music provided by McKee's Band between 7 p.m. and 9 p.m.

The building was then taken over by Ann Street Brewery who turned the ballroom into living quarters. The gallery room was rented by the Boy's Brigade who met every Thursday night, and the band would practice once other business had been concluded. On Sunday mornings, at 10.45 a.m., the Brigade would gather outside the Queen's Assembly Rooms, play a few rousing marches, then proceed up Ann Street for the 11 o'clock service at St James' Church. Eventually numbers dwindled and the Gallery Room was turned into a store.

ROCQUEBERG

THE great rock known as Rocqueberg near Green Island, standing 40 feet high, has always had a cold, dark, foreboding atmosphere for any passer-by. Even today, surrounded by a circle of trees which prevents any sunlight falling on the rock, it has the appearance of a place of evil. It is easy to understand why our ancestors kept well away from this place, especially on nights when there was a full moon.

Many stories of witches using Rocqueberg to hold their sabbaths have been handed down through the ages. Two hundred years ago it must have been an extremely isolated headland and ideal for a witches' coven to meet and practice its evil art.

Two stories, found in many local history books, tell of the work of witches during the 17th and 18th centuries. The first concerns a young fisherman called Hurbert who was engaged to be married to a young girl named Madalaine. After taking her home each night he would stroll along past Rocqueberg, and the great rock aroused his curiosity in witchcraft. One evening he witnessed some beautiful maidens dancing around the rock, and was approached by one who invited him to join them the following night. When Madalaine heard the story she feared for her fiancé and sought advice from the parish priest. He gave her a cross, telling her that if she wished to save his soul from the Devil she must follow Hurbert and use the crucifix against the forces of evil.

The witches' haunt of Rocqueberg.

That night she kept her appointment at Rocqueberg and found Hurbert surrounded by haggard old witches who danced around him. He was under their spell and saw them as beautiful young girls, but Madaline held her cross and could see the witches in their true light. She raised the cross above her head and threw it at the witches. Hurbert was immediately brought out of his trance and the witches disappeared with shrieks of terror. The couple left Rocqueberg and never again were troubled with witchcraft.

The second story tells of how the witches would conjure up great storms when fishermen were passing Rocqueberg on their way home with their catches of fish. On hearing the witches singing, the fishermen had to give them every 13th fish or else the storm would wreck their boats and drown all on board. Their reign of terror was broken by one young man who refused to comply with their demands. As he sailed through the stormy water the witches began singing. He held aloft a five rayed starfish, cut off one ray and threw the fish into their midst shouting: "The cross is my passport." The fish, in the shape of a cross, landed on the witches and they never again appeared at Rocqueberg point.

Today Rocqueberg is part of a private residence and visitors can only sit in their coach whilst the driver slows down and points out the landmark, telling them that the imprint of a cloven hoof can still be found in the rock which once was the meeting place of the witches of Jersey.

THE BATTLE OF THE OYSTER SHELLS

OYSTERS have always been regarded as a delicacy by the French. Magical powers have been attributed to the oyster as an aphrodisiac. If the powers of this sought-after shell fish are true, then due to the large oyster fishing industry which existed on our eastern coast during the first half of the 1800s, our ancestors may be correct in blaming the oyster for the many large families in Jersey at that period!

In 1797, a few miles off the north east coast of Chausey, a large bank of oysters was discovered. A few local fishermen took advantage of this new industry, and whilst there was only a minimal intrusion, the French apparently turned a blind eye. There had always been an agreed limit of one league from the coast of France as far as fishing rights were concerned, and as the main bank of oysters was outside this limit, the few local boats were left alone. By 1810 all this had altered, with the few boats having multiplied many times over — the Jersey oyster fishing boom had started.

During the following ten years the number of boats grew to 300, with the majority coming from England. With a six-man crew for each vessel, this meant 1,800 seamen involved, plus a further 1,000 land workers. These were mainly people from the eastern parishes of St Clement, Grouville and St Martin. The oyster dredging season lasted from September 1st until June 1st, although the most profitable period was between February and May. The main port for the boats was Gorey, with smaller fleets using Bouley Bay, Rozel and La Rocque.

The French didn't take kindly to this mass assault on their oyster beds by foreign fishermen, and the principals of the port of Granville were instrumental in calling upon gun boats to patrol the oyster beds. Numerous incidents occurred with these armed vessels making many attacks on the local fishing fleet during 1821 and 1822.

In 1824, Prince de Polignac, the French Ambassador to the Court in London, proposed the fishing limits be extended to two leagues, and where the banks were most abundant, to three leagues. These measures were finally agreed upon, much to the dismay of the fishing population. They had for some time been receiving an armed escort up to one league from the French coast. Now the English warships had to pull back to the new boundaries. Many fishermen refused to accept the new limits and continued to fish the banks of oysters at the places where they were most abundant. Many of these boats were fired upon and some were taken into custody, with the crews being thrown into prison or flogged before being released on condition they never again entered French waters. A number of captains continued to run the gauntlet with the French gun boats by dredging at night. However, smaller catches were recorded and the French were once again able to sell oysters to the English market at a cheaper price than the locally-based boats.

The States had spent a great deal of money at Gorey and wanted the industry to continue. From a small village, Gorey had grown into one of the most important and financially productive parts of Jersey. £16,000 had been spent on the original pier and the States were in the process of extending it. A shipyard had been constructed as well as dozens of cottages and a church — with services being delivered in English in accordance with the wishes of the many visiting fishermen — plus a school which catered for the educational needs of their children. With all this capital being ploughed into Gorey, the States of Jersey needed a solution to the problem, and ordered the Committee of Piers and Harbours to deliver a report on the oyster fishing trade which they presented to the States on January 28th, 1834.

The fishermen were also trying to safeguard their livelihood by controlling the price of oysters. The average price paid by the merchants was three shillings and six pence (17½p) for a three bushel tub, although this price constantly fluctuated between three and four shillings. Any offer lower than three shillings would see the captains refusing to leave port, and an iron chain was fastened across the pier to prevent anyone breaking the strike. They also subsidised their income by landing a good supply of lobsters for the tables of the English gentry.

One of the recommendations of the committee was for an oyster bed to be laid in the Bay of Grouville, therefore allowing the fishermen trouble-free dredging for the shellfish. This was adopted by the States, who spent £3,866 between 1834 and 1837 on seed oysters. When these beds were opened in 1837, only certain parts could be dredged at one time, allowing the oysters to breed and grow to over 2½ inches across the shell, which was the official size they had to have reached before they could be gathered. Inspectors using wooden measuring gauges were employed to see that this law was enforced.

Certain captains disregarded the law and took their boats into the reserved banks. At first only a few broke into the restricted areas of oysters until, on April 12th, 1838, a large number of boats put to sea and dredged a restricted bank. The Constables of Grouville and St Martin notified the Lieutenant-Governor, Major-General Campbell, who accompanied the St Helier Battalion of the Militia, the 60th Regiment from Fort Regent, plus a unit of artillery, to Gorey.

Major-General Campbell took command of the operation from a vantage point on top of the castle and ordered the artillery to open fire on the boats. Whether the distance was too great or they were poor marksmen is uncertain, because no direct hit was made and no-one was injured. The fishermen gave in immediately, and 96 skippers were arrested by the Deputy Viscount Mr Godfray, placed on bail and later fined £17. 6s. 2d. each. Only the two ringleaders were detained in prison for trial.

Oyster fishing boats at Gorey, 1849.

The incident became known as the Battle of the Oyster Shells with the only real victim being Major-General Campbell. Whilst controlling his troops from the exposed heights of the castle, he caught a chill and was confined to his bed where he died on May 12th.

The oyster industry never really recovered from being banned from French waters and the following battle with the Militia. Some boats continued the uphill struggle until 1871, when the oyster fishermen disappeared to new banks.

In August 1974, Mr J. P. Le Garignon and Mr J. Le Mene attempted to revive the industry off La Rocque when they laid 100,000 seed oysters, although their efforts didn't materialise into the financial proportions required to make it a viable proposition.

Gorey has now been taken over by the tourist industry, and the fleet of oysters boats has gone forever, giving way to pleasure craft and boats transporting hundreds of welcome visitors to and from the now friendly and hospitable French waters.

GREVE DE LECQ

DURING the 19th century Jersey had a vast fishing fleet. The numerous boats needed harbours in which to dock whilst unloading their catches and when repairs were required. Also when the seas became rough during stormy weather, the boats had to scurry for the nearest moorings. More harbours were needed on the north coast of the Island, and many fishermen felt that Greve de Lecq would make a suitable point for anchorage.

The States of Jersey formed a committee on March 14th, 1864. Their task was to draw up the plans for a harbour and to ascertain the cost of such a project.

The committee finally came back to the States and the decision to construct the harbour was made on June 22nd, 1866. The contractor for the difficult task was Philippe Amy of L'Etacq, who enlisted the help of a 40-strong workforce.

Everything moved slowly, and the time between the States deciding to act and the laying of the foundation stone was almost six years. Jurat J. J. Aubin finally laid the stone on May 7th, 1872. The Rector of St Ouen then read a long prayer in French, after which all the dignitaries present walked to the Greve de Lecq Hotel which was under the patronage of Mr Poujol. There the assembled party was treated to a seven course dinner consisting of soup, a

Greve de Lecq's harbour.

Storm damage wrecked the pier in 1879.

fish course, meat with vegetables, plum pudding, fruit, grapes and coffee. An ample supply of wine helped to wash down the banquet, and numerous brandies were drunk with the coffee. This was followed by a fireworks display at 8 p.m., after which everyone retired to their homes leaving Philippe Amy's men to begin their task the following morning.

In January 1879 the pier was still under construction when it was severely damaged by a storm. Eventually the work was completed, although it was to have a short life. Whilst arguments were taking place between the States and the builder, who was demanding more money than had originally been put aside, another great storm on February 21st, 1885, demolished most of the remaining pier.

Engineers sent to inspect the harbour found there had been many structural faults, and with the cost of rebuilding being astronomically high, it was decided to abandon the project.

For years the pier remained a pile of rubble with the sea constantly breaking over the heap of rocks and causing a great deal of erosion on the beach. It was many years before the great stones were made safe, and all ideas of turning Greve de Lecq into a safe harbour have certainly been abandoned forever.

PIERRE LE SUEUR AND THE BREAD RIOTS

PIERRE LE SUEUR was born on November 20th, 1811, in St Helier where he later studied law and became an Advocate of the Royal Court. When Pierre Perrot was elevated from the position of Constable of St Helier to that of Jurat on November 9th, 1839, the unanimous decision of all concerned was to elect Pierre Le Sueur as Constable of the Parish.

He commenced his first term of office on November 18th when he was only 28-years-old, and soon became one of the most popular Constables for many years. He had a soft, yet clear and concise manner of speaking and his knowledge of the law of Jersey helped him win numerous debates. He was instrumental in organising the town's sewerage system — many houses still had sewers which opened straight onto the streets. He also helped in forming a fire brigade, cleared many of the slums and came up with the idea of numbering all the houses in each street, beginning with the end closest to the Royal Square, a system which is still in use today.

Due to these and numerous other good deeds to the parish, he was honoured with a presentation of a magnificent collection of silverware which is now on display in the Town Hall. Pierre Le Sueur was re-elected as Constable in 1842, for a third term on December 6th, 1845, again on December 16th, 1848, and finally on January 10th, 1852. His term as Father of the Parish ended suddenly on January 16th, 1853, when, due to overwork, he collapsed and died of a heart attack at the age of 41. A memorial was built opposite his birthplace in Broad Street as a permanent reminder of this quiet, bespectacled man who had accomplished so much for his parish. The inscription reads: "This monument was erected by his grateful fellow citizens to Peter Le Sueur."

One of his most unsavoury tasks during his years at the helm was in helping to quell the Bread Riots of 1847.

There had been a great deal of unemployment during the early 18th century, and therefore labour was cheap. The average wage was only two shillings per day, and the farmers were receiving a higher income by exporting the majority of their crops, so the locals were having to pay high prices for potatoes and other vegetables. Bread was also expensive, with a 4 lb loaf costing one shilling. Many workers were finding it increasingly difficult to feed their families, and the first stirrings of trouble amongst the lower paid and unemployed was felt in January 1847.

To combat the problem the States decided on February 1st to commence baking bread for the poor in the ovens of the General Hospital for only two pence a pound. Work was also created when the States hired many labourers to finish St Aubin's Road. With less unemployment, the bakers increased the

The old Robin Hood Tavern beseiged during the Bread Riots of 1847.

price of bread as they felt people were now earning more money. The same reason was given in April by the States when they ceased baking cheap bread.

Then ships were sabotaged whilst loading their cargo of locally grown produce. The police were helpless to stop these acts, which also included the seizure of farmers' goods on the way to the pier. Matters grew steadily worse until the climax came on Monday, May 17th.

The men working on St Aubin's Road were the first to down tools and march towards Town. They were joined by the shipwrights of the Deslandes yard at First Tower, and on reaching St Helier they made a tour of the Town until the initial group of workers had become a mob over 1,000 strong. Their confidence had grown with their size, and the leaders decided to march the army of angry workers to the Town Mills.

The Mills were situated alongside the stream running down Grands Vaux from Mont Neron to where the Caesarean Lawn Tennis Club now stands. The Town Mills were owned by the Le Quesne family who had purchased the entire collection of mills from Francois Jeune in 1835. The miller was a man called Pellier, and the mob vented their anger on this unfortunate man by chanting: "Cheaper bread or Pellier's head; Cheaper Flour or Pellier's last hour."

Centenier Le Bailly tried to reason with them without any success. The workers broke into the mills doing a vast amount of damage, then loaded 17 sacks of wheat and flour onto two carts which had been left nearby.

Lieutenant Colonel Cregh, who was in command of the 81st Regiment stationed at Fort Regent, was ordered to take sufficient troops to quell the riot. The mob were returning from the mills with the two loaded carts when, at 2.30 p.m. they reached the Robin Hood Tavern where they were met by Constable Pierre Le Sueur. He climbed on board the first cart and read the riot act to the crowd. The mob listened to this popular man and the drivers released the reigns and climbed down from the horse drawn carts. At this point the soldiers arrived and many of the mob began to disperse. The leaders were taken into the tavern, although some were able to escape out of the unguarded side door. The remainder were sentenced to a term in prison on a diet of bread and water.

The riot achieved its desired effect, because the States once again produced bread at 2d a pound compared to the bakers 3½d a pound. Constable Le Sueur started a fund for the poor which soon reached the total of £715.

The Bread Riot was over and Pierre Le Sueur was able to return to his duties as Constable in which his main aim was to help the poor of the parish. His untimely death brought Nicholas Le Quesne to the position of Father of the capital of Jersey. Although Pierre Le Sueur accomplished many good deeds during his term of office, he will always be remembered for something he tried hard to help avoid — the Bread Riots of 1847.

The monument to Pierre Le Sueur in Broad Street

CROIX DE LA BATAILLE

PERO (PEDRO) NINO, Count of Buelna, was born in Castile, Spain in 1378. He was trained in combat as befitted the son of a nobleman, and at the age of 25 had a small fleet of ships under his command. He attacked many small ports in the south of France before sailing to the north coast where he joined forces with Charles de Savoisy.

With their combined fleet they set sail for England where they attacked numerous ports on the south coast, including Poole and Portsmouth. Pero's first visit to the Channel Islands was on his return from this voyage, when he stopped off at Alderney before returning to France and wintering in Rouen.

Croix de la Bataille.

He then joined forces with a Breton Knight, Pierre de Pontbriand, whose surname was Hector. Together they plotted an attack on Jersey, intent on plundering the Island and obtaining as much booty as possible, in addition to hostages they could hold to ransom.

Although many accounts of the following assault on Jersey placed Pero as the leader of the attackers, thanks to Pero's lieutenant and standard bearer, Gutierre Diaz de Gamez, who wrote of the many exploits of his master, and papers in the National Archives in Paris, the true facts of this invasion can be told. Pierre de Pontbriand was the real figurehead, and it was he who supplied most of the army of 1,000 men, mainly Bretons and Normans, putting Pero in charge of his small band of Castilians.

On October 7th, 1406, they set sail from France, landing at the Hermitage of St Helier at night on a high tide. The following morning after the tide had receded, the invaders marched across the sand where they were met by 3,000 men-at-arms under the direction of Sir John Pykworth and a captain who was known as the Receiver. A fierce battle took place with neither side gaining an overall advantage, until Pero Nino rallied 50 of his men and cried: "So long as the banner of St George is on high, so long will these English fight." He then led his small band of men towards the Standard, capturing it and killing the Receiver.

The local troops retreated with the fall of their leader and Standard, although the invaders were too exhausted after the prolonged battle to give chase. They retired back across the sands to their anchorage whilst the local troops retreated to Gorey Castle.

The following morning the invaders held a council of war. News had reached them that the English fleet was approaching the Island and the locals were entrenched in the numerous castles and earthen fortifications. Many wanted to collect what loot they could find and leave Jersey before the arrival of the English fleet. Pero knew that whoever held the main castle at Gorey controlled the Island, and he persuaded the army to advance on the castle, burning all before them. On reaching the heights of Grouville they were met by the English and Jersey forces where another battle took place.

Once again this confrontation was proving inconclusive when a Herald appeared from Gorey Castle. He was accompanied by some prominent Islanders who offered a ransom if the invaders would return to France. After much discussion a ransom of 10,000 gold crowns was agreed. Permission was granted for the release of about 30 French prisoners, and they also took four hostages who would only be released when the remainder of the ransom was paid, as the full amount could not be raised at such short notice.

The place of this confrontation was christened by the locals "Croix de la Bataille," and the small hill which ran alongside the main path to Gorey became known as Blood Hill due to the amount of blood which dripped onto the ground from the bodies of the dead and wounded as they were carried back to the safety of the castle.

The band of invaders made their way back to their ships, collecting as many horses and cows as they could find on the way. The hostages were later sold to merchants of Brittany for the remainder of the ransom which was equally divided between all the men.

All that remains of this battle is a small plot of land situated at the top of Grouville Hill and a stone epitaph to the many men who laid down their lives for their Island.

ST SAVIOUR'S HOSPITAL

DURING the 1840s, the States of Jersey became aware of the growing number of patients at the General Hospital who were being treated for mental illness. A letter dated January 13th, 1847, from the States to Whitehall, explained the need for a building for the treatment of persons inflicted with insanity. The land which the States wanted to use was part of Queen's Farm in St Saviour, which the Crown finally let for a nominal rent.

Tenders were invited for the building of the Mental Hospital and Messrs Benest and Pirouet were appointed contractors. Their tender for the main building was £5,980, with an additional £180 for arching over the corridors

The impressive façade of St Saviour's Hospital.

and single sleeping accommodation, plus £150 for the installation of two large cisterns. This made a total of £6,310, which is a far cry from the £2 million spent on the addition to St Saviour's called Redwood House. This unit, opened in November 1984, has 60 beds and caters for psycho-geriatric patients.

The foundation stone of St Saviour's Hospital was laid at 4 p.m. on Thursday, July 27th, 1865, by the Lieutenant-Governor of Jersey, Major-General Burke-Cuppage. Also present were the Lord Bishop of Peterborough, the Very Rev. the Dean of Jersey, members of the States and other public officials, including Philip Le Gallais, who was president of the Committee of the States for the building of what was then called the 'LUNATIC ASYLUM'.

The Jersey Lunatic Asylum opened its doors on Saturday, July 11th, 1868, when Mr Jackson, who had been appointed in charge, welcomed six men and six women from the ward at the General Hospital as the first patients. A law was passed in 1890 allowing doctors to certify people as mentally insane. Once admitted to the Asylum, only a discharge from the Public Health Committee, or more probably death, would gain their release from the institution.

During the 19th century and the early half of the 20th century, treatment of mental illness was still in its infancy. Today a caring, well-trained staff, with all the latest equipment and medicine, treats patients as the fellow human beings they are. Every effort is made towards rehabilitation into the outside world, with lessons in cookery, general skills and trades, including computer courses. During the opening years of the hospital none of these facilities were available, and patients were locked away from humanity where their families could forget they ever existed.

Extensions to the Asylum were added in 1891 and 1911 as the number of patients grew and more beds were required. After the building in 1911, some 230 patients could be housed, and the main building has remained structurally unchanged up to the present time.

The name Lunatic Asylum was used right up until 1952, when it was changed to the Jersey Mental Hospital. The public were still fairly ignorant of the happenings behind the locked doors, and the stigma attached to mental illness remained. In an effort to combat this feeling, the name was again changed in 1963 to St Saviour's Hospital.

A new law, which came into force on January 1st, 1972, changed many of the outdated rules of admission, and since then great strides have been made in the treatment of patients. Modern buildings such as the Clinique Pinel, Orchard House and Maison des Vaux have been incorporated into the hospital complex. Today, a total of 304 beds are usually available. There is approximately an equal number of male and female patients, with beds provided for children. These youngsters are housed in a modern unit called Cherry Lodge which opened in 1974.

Staff at the hospital now outnumber patients. A total of 327 people work in the various units of the complex. There are 229 nurses, 80 auxiliary staff, 29 medical officers and nine administration posts. The head of the hospital is called the Senior Nursing Officer, as opposed to the older term of Matron.

Many outside bodies have taken a practical interest in the well-being of the patients over the past 20 years. The Sixth Form Society of Jersey's schools have been visiting for at least 18 years, putting on shows and taking an interest in the children's unit. The Jersey Association of Mental Health formed a group known as the Friends of St Saviour's, who can always be relied upon at Christmas and birthdays, arriving with arms full of presents. They also organise day trips in their cars and visit those patients who have no living relatives. The Lions Club donated the profits from their 1974 Swimarathon to the building of an indoor swimming pool, which is well used by patients of all ages.

The hospital also arranges holidays, with trips to England and France being the most popular. Two parties of children have visited Butlin's Holiday Camp at Minehead, and the adults have an exchange scheme with a hospital at St Lo in France. Alternate years see six patients, accompanied by two members of staff, visit this up-to-date hospital, where the emphasis is on entertainment with a special officer responsible for providing both day and night-time activities. Also numerous day-trips to France, Guernsey and Sark, plus outings at many of Jersey's top restaurants help the patients to lead as active and normal a life as possible.

Those who are being rehabilitated for a return to the outside world often have full or part-time jobs and only return to their unit at the hospital for their meals and a night's sleep. Short-term patients are now kept at a special ward in the General Hospital. Recreations such as football, cricket, woodwork, handicraft and pottery are among the many outlets provided to help pass the long hours for those who will spend the remainder of their days within the confines of the hospital grounds.

Many changes, nearly always for the better, have been made since 1868. Mental illness is no longer looked upon by society as something that should be locked away out of sight. Much of the old stigma has been removed since the days when St Saviour's Hospital was known by the awesome title of the Jersey Lunatic Asylum.

OCCUPATION STAMPS

SINCE the introduction of the postage stamp, the Channel Islands had, until the Second World War, relied upon Britain for its supply of stamps. The idea of producing local stamps had never been considered until the German Occupation made the authorities of both main Islands carry out a complete re-appraisal of the situation.

The English stamps of the period were a definitive issue of King George VI which first came out in 1937, and the recently arrived Postal Centenary Issue depicting both Queen Victoria and King George VI, which went on sale on May 6th, 1940. The fact that the Germans arrived just six weeks after the Centenary Issue meant that larger than normal stock was to be found in the Post Office.

With 10,000 letters being posted each week, the supply of these stamps was soon greatly reduced. Postage within the Island at the time cost 1d, and the depletion in stocks of this stamp caused the Acting-Postmaster, Mr H.C. Chappell, to enlist the aid of the Bailiff of Guernsey, Victor G. Carey, in producing the format for the first Guernsey stamps.

But before this idea could be finalised, the stock of stamps became exhausted. The Germans suggested bisecting the 2d stamp and approval was obtained from H.M. Post Office. The following notice appeared in both the *Evening Press* and *The Star* on December 24th, 1940.

> "The Post Office advises that further supplies of 1d postage stamps are not at present available and that, until further notice, prepayment of penny postage (for printed papers, etc) can be effected by using one half of a 2d stamp, provided that division is made by cutting the stamp diagonally. It is emphasised that the bisection of stamps should be done carefully and that correspondence bearing half stamps not cut in the manner indicated will be liable to surcharge."

First day covers of the 2d bisect were not available until December 27th, due to the closure of the Post Office over the Christmas period. It is estimated that approximately 120,000 of the Centenary Issue were bisected, along with 40,000 of the King George VI definitive issue. Also a few thousand 2d stamps of King George were bisected.

Many of the occupying forces were keen philatelists and, along with local collectors, placed a great demand on the Post Office. Guernsey's first postage stamps were issued on Tuesday February 18th, 1941, and the bisect stamp ceased to be legal on Saturday February 22nd, having had a life of only 58 days. The 2d orange stamp faded from use, although it was to become a collectors item in the years ahead.

Guernsey was the first Channel Island to issue its own stamps because Jersey had a larger stock of British stamps at the outset of the Occupation. Designed by E.W. Vaudin and printed by the Guernsey Press, the stamps depicted the coat of arms with the words "Guernsey Postage". The 1d scarlet stamp went on sale on February 18th, 1941, followed by the ½d green on April 7th of the same year. This was followed on April 12th, 1944, with the 2½d ultramarine stamp. Shortage of paper caused some stamps to be produced on French water-marked paper which, during the gumming process, turned blue. This was due to the presence of a certain amount of oil in the gum being used, and these stamps were so sought after by collectors that they quickly sold out. The ½d only lasted from March 11th until March 31st, 1942, while the 1d stamp came out on April 7th and was sold out by April 25th.

Numerous variations of shades can be found, and problems with the cutters caused differences with the perforations. During March and April of 1945, all stocks of stamps had been used up, and a meter franking machine was used until the liberation of Guernsey.

Jersey issued its first stamp on April 1st, 1941. This was the 1d scarlet with the bright green ½d stamp going on sale on January 29th, 1942. Both stamps were designed by Major N.V.L. Rybot and printed by the Jersey Evening Post. They were of similar design to the Guernsey stamps, and due to shortage of

95

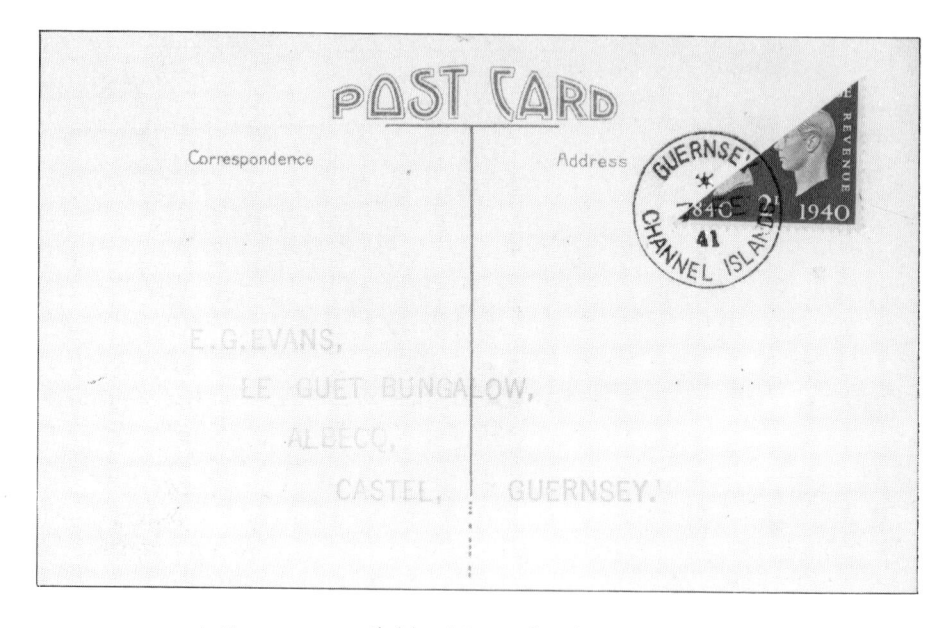

paper were, at times, unavailable. Meter franking was used during one of these periods from May until August 1942. All the stamps produced locally had no watermarks and were printed on white paper.

Following a suggestion by the Germans, the States asked Edmund Blampied, the famous painter, to design a set of 6 pictorial stamps. The result was a beautiful set of stamps with the ½d green showing an old Jersey farm, and 480,000 of these were printed The 1d scarlet depicted Portelet Bay and 840,000 were issued. Both these stamps came on sale on June 1st, 1943. On June 8th, the 1½d brown with a drawing of Corbière Lighthouse, and a sketch of Elizabeth Castle on the 2d orange/yellow came on the market, and 360,000 of each of these stamps were issued. The 2½d blue of Mont Orgueil Castle and the 3d violet with the famous scene of the gathering of vraic followed on June 29th. 720,000 copies of the 2½d stamp and 360,000 of the 3d stamp were printed.

The French government undertook the task of producing this set of stamps with the engraved plates being made by Monsieur Henri Cortot. They were printed at the works of Postes, Telegraphs et Telephones in Paris and have always been immensely popular with collectors. The 1d and 2½d issues were also produced on newsprint.

Today, the Island enjoy a large revenue from the sale of local stamps, with collectors from all over the world placing orders at the philatelic bureau. Many sets have come on the market since the Islands took over the local Post Offices, although none of the modern stamps hold as much value or memories as the stamps issued during the German Occupation.